Strictly Confidential!

CF FOR HELP

GW00645477

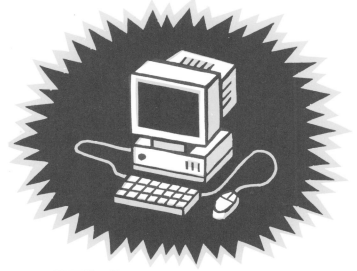

36 Scam E-mails from Africa
illustrated by Henning Wagenbreth
Gingko Press

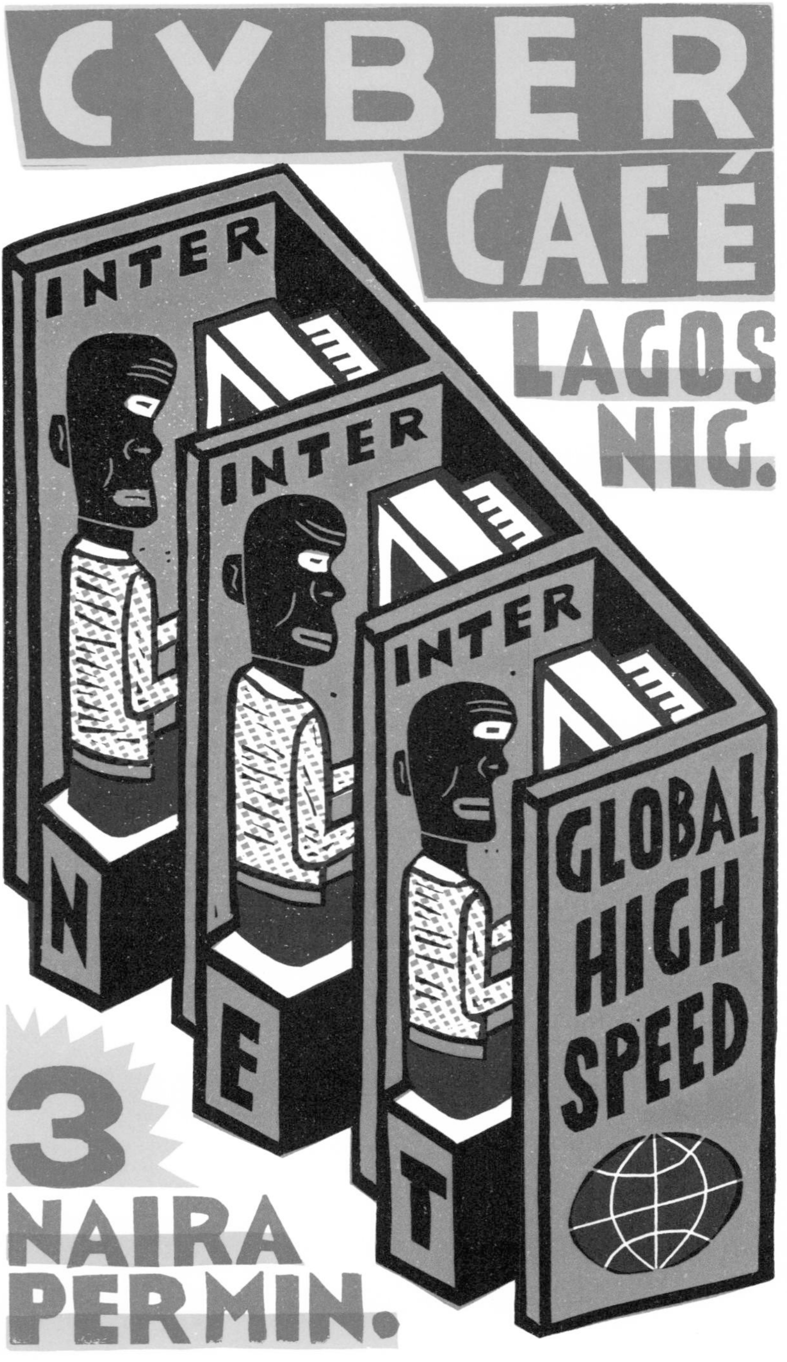
CYBER
CAFÉ
LAGOS
NIG.
INTER
INTER
INTER
N
E
T
GLOBAL
HIGH
SPEED
3
NAIRA
PER MIN.

Dollars, Gold and Diamonds
E-mails from Africa

Perhaps the world can still be saved! Repentant Islamic guerillas return plundered goods to Christian communities. Rich orphans desperately seek adoptive parents. Win a fortune in Lotto without even playing! Government employees make the world more peaceful by pocketing millions of dollars that are meant to be used to buy weapons. Suitcases filled with dyed US dollars delivered free of charge to your home. The money needs only to be washed.

Since the beginning of 1990's, scam-mails from Africa have been reporting such remarkable events as these. Skepticism follows the initial astonishment. The promises would of course be wonderful were they true. In contrast to the so-called spam-mails that offer cheap services in undesirable mass advertising and are simply annoying, scam-mails aim to be especially deceitful. The African scam-mails differ from other fraudulent e-mails in their creativity, audacity and their ludicrous claims. They are fancifully written and thrilling to read. There are no passwords guilefully requested in an attempt to grab a few dollars. Here we're talking millions. In grand style the swindlers promise heaven and earth to get foreigners to voluntarily hand over piles of cash.

The deception with scam-mails works in the following way: first the scammers locate appropriate e-mail address suppliers and buy thousands of addresses of people all over the world, especially those people from rich, industrial nations. Enticing letters are then written and sent as mass e-mails. The author asserts that he has come upon too much money either through legitimate inheritance, political unrest, a tragic accident or through simple theft. In telling his plausible story, he slips into one of various roles decorated with rich detail. Sometimes it's

You greedy thieves have to pay for Centuries of Slave Trade!

the helpless child by his parent's deathbed who's received millions of dollars and doesn't know what to do with it all. Another time he may pose as the government official who is manipulating the state budget or embezzling state funds and is in search of someone to help launder the money. Or he pretends to be the relative of a deposed dictator and authoritatively demands immediate assistance with a foreign currency transfer.

The tone of the letters is cleverly chosen; it's at times subservient, condescending, solicitous or disdainful. The political, geographic and temporal facts are always on the mark. Internet links to serious news web sites are provided to convince the skeptics. Furthermore, all scam-mails have something in common: the alleged multimillionaires have anxiety that they will lose their newfound riches due to the uncertain nature of African affairs and, therefore, desperately need help and are searching for a partner to provide bank account information for an immediate transfer of millions of dollars.

The recipient of such a scam-mail is at first puzzled that an African has come upon his e-mail address. He doesn't know that thousands of others have received the same letter. He is assured that he has been carefully selected as a potential business partner. The description of a tragic accident awakens his compassion and the tale of large-scale corruption confirms his prejudice making the story believable: Africa is indeed rich and beautiful but also wild and chaotic. The awareness of his civilizing advantage sways the recipient to certainty. That to-morrow could bring at least a seven-figure sum to his bank account captivates him, blurring his judgment. The commission alone would make him a millionaire. The opportunity is one-of-a-kind: there's no risk and the gain is astronomical. There is no business more lucrative. Thus, the name, address and account number are sent to the African fraudster. He thanks him and promises to promptly handle all the formalities. However, there are difficulties: a million dollar sum is not so easy to send across the world. There are bank fees, a lawyer must prepare the agreement, and perhaps there are customs officials to bribe. The swindler cannot muster these fees alone and begs his »business partner« for an advance from the expected high return. Once this money has been transferred from the recipient's account, he never hears from the swindler again. The criminal term for this ploy is »advanced fee fraud«.

One likes to laugh at the naïveté of the swindled but the African scam-mails have wreaked millions of dollars of damage. In relevant internet forums victims from various countries complain of great financial losses. Several have ruined their livelihoods and are contemplating suicide. An English state treasurer who wanted to increase the wealth of his parish was conned out of the public funds to

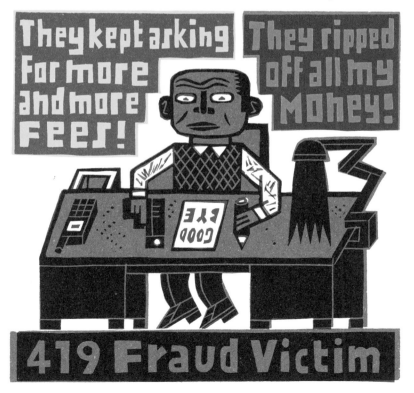

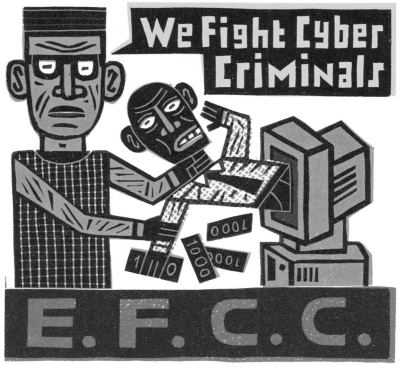

which his was entrusted. Business people who were lured to Africa to conclude the agreement were robbed and abused. And the estimated number of unreported cases is high. Who goes to the police when he has been defrauded during an illegal business deal?

The FBI and European police departments advise against responding to such letters. The Nigerian mafia is considered the source. It has spread from Lagos to become the most organized crime network in Africa. Its influence reaches as far as Europe and the U.S. Alongside drug dealing, slave trading and white-collar crime, con-letters form a business sector known as the »Nigeria Connection«. Since the 1980's, scam-letters have been sent, first by post and then later by fax, to small- and medium-sized businesses. The internet has provided a more cost effective method of solicitation and has therefore created a much wider distribution of scam-letters. If only a small fraction of recipients is convinced to give money, the cost is well worth the effort. The distribution of fraud-mail has become the largest Nigerian industry after oil and cocoa exports.

The Nigerian government learned long ago that advanced fee fraud harms the state's reputation. The swindled money is used again to bribe public officials thus undermining the whole political system. President Olusegun Obasanjo founded the »Economic and Financial Crimes Commission« (EFFC). Advanced fee fraud was added to Nigeria's Criminal Code Act under article 419 that states that a violator may be incarcerated for up to seven years. Because there's very little trust in banks within Nigeria, money is most often transferred in cash, making it very difficult to trace these criminal offences. But the cheated parties are also guilty within this system of fraud. Their claim that the African criminals should be locked away is exceedingly hypocritical as it is their cooperation and their voluntary prepayments that allow the criminal scheme to function. In the meantime, Transparency International has intervened. This organization to combat international corruption demands that victims of prepayment fraud also pay a fine equal to the amount of their lost money because they are participating in the theft of public funds.

The African swindlers feel justified in fleecing their victims. They are only stealing back from the whites that which was stolen from them during centuries of slavery and colonialism. This line of reasoning is a cheap justification for the underhanded behavior but does contain a kernel of truth. Africa had long been ruthlessly exploited and since independence, the former colonies have fared little better. For the industrialized nations of the world the former colonies are little more than a sales market for subsidized foodstuffs and other consumer goods. The European and North American markets remain African producers but closed ones. This global imbalance creates poverty. Because there is so little hope of improvement, ever more Africans are looking north for work. Under life-threatening conditions they set off on their journey only to find heightened borders and intensified immigration laws. Most of those who manage to succeed in making the trip live illegally and are easy prey for cheap labor.

Because of this injustice, one can develop sympathy for these scam-artists (as they are so called on many web sites.) In artful and scheming ways they take from the rich and give to the poor, a bit like the Robin Hood of lore. With the help of the internet and great creativity they manage to cross the closely guarded north-south border and write money out of people's pockets. They keenly play with our latent racism and bad colonial conscience. The authors are familiar with western culture and the western mind set and they play dumb. Many of their convoluted stories read like old folk tales telling of good and evil kings, of golden treasures, of princes and princesses. Like folklore in preliterate times, the same scam-mail stories circulate in many different versions; only this time, they are retold electronically and embellished with the appropriate details.

Many e-mail-users in recent years have received African scam-mails. Several have responded to them, most have laughed at them and almost all have went ahead and deleted them. It would be a shame if they were entirely lost, depicting as they do in tragicomic manner the contemporary facets of the north-south conflict and how easily a technological invention like the internet, that weapon of globalization, can be turned against its creators. From the plenitude of scam-mails 36 will be selected, illustrated and published in this book.

Henning Wagenbreth

From: Danladi Abacha <damab@onebox.com>
Date: Saturday, March 2, 2002, 15:44:22
Subject: urgent assistance needed

DON'T HESITATE!

I am Mr. Danladi Abacha. The third son of late General Sani Abacha, former Nigerian head of state. In May last year the present democratic government of President Olusegun Obasanjo sent security men to my most elderly brother's Mohammed house and recovered about seven hundred million dollars (U.S.$700 million) cash kept in house by my late father.

Visit this site http://www.transparency.org/documents/newsletter/2000.3reforms.html and read the story for confirmation. Also 3.6 billion pounds sterling in a London account and the 2.2 billion naira in a Nigeria account were frozen and our properties confiscated including our business empires, traveling documents confiscated.

My brother in jail and my mother under house arrest. The security men are also after me and I have U.S.$10 million money hidden somewhere. Now I want to move the money cash to abroad quickly as government investigators are hunting for me to recover the money.

Due to my present predicament I am soliciting to entrust this money in your custody until this trial period of my family is over. For your assistance I will give you 30% of the total money as soon as I reach a compromise with you.

I shall inform you of the security company and shipment modality via diplomatic means when I receive your consent. Please don't hesitate to assist me, because I am very much in need of your help.
Thanks in anticipation.

Yours truly,
Danladi Abacha

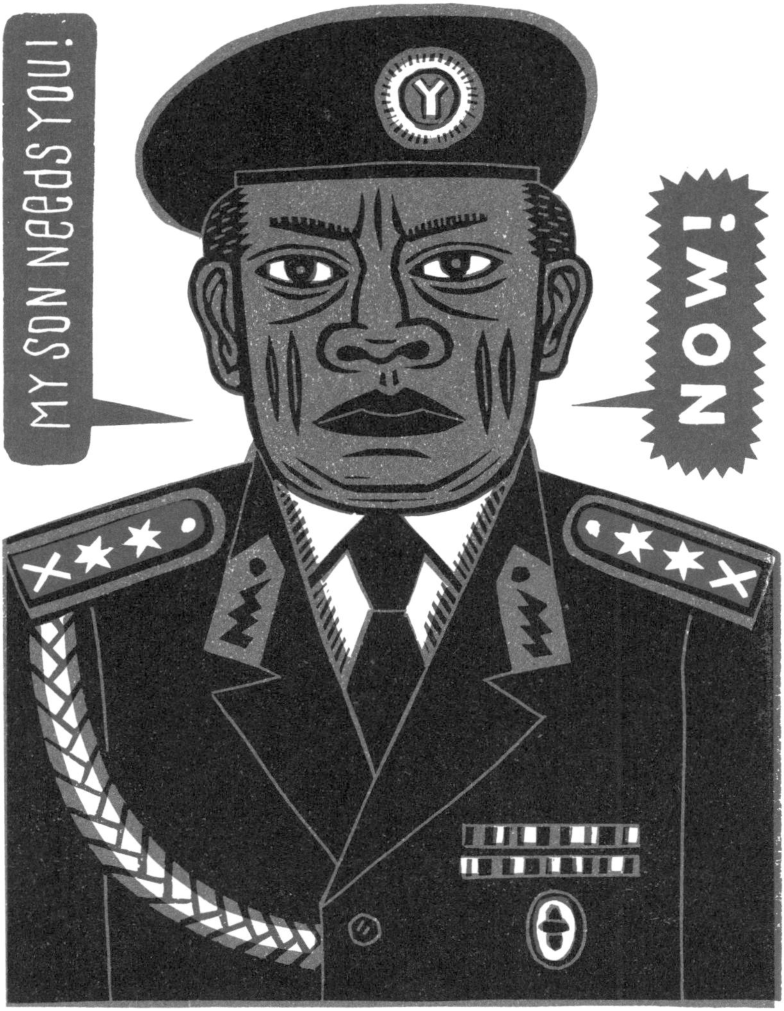

★ General ★
Sani Abacha

From: Abba Abacha <abbah37@epatra.com>
Date: Friday, April 5, 2002, 01:31:20
Subject: private!

PRIVATE!

Good day,

this might seem very deplorable for a person that you do not know but as the title implies I am Abba Abacha, the second son of the late General Sani Abacha. I got your contact from our Chamber of Commerce in their international directory and I am contacting you due to the present situation as regards the special panel set up by the present democratic administration in my country (Nigeria) under the anti-corruption law passed mainly to recover what they termed »Abacha's looted money«. This law is yet another smear campaign aimed mainly to frustrate, humiliate, dismember and widen the scope of hatred to our family. A personal vendetta by President Obasanjo who was jailed by my father's government for plotting a coup d'etat against his administration.

This highly calculated attempt by this administration cum Swiss government through bilateral relationship has taken away from us over U.S.$1.4 billion in Switzerland. The rampaging situation in our accounts abroad has yielded to the barbaric pressure and just last month we were squished out of another U.S.$395 million and all this funds can be ascertained independently. You may wish to confirm this from a leading newspaper in Nigeria (This Day) from their web site at www.thisdayonline.com from the archives section in the March 10, 2001, January 26, 2002 and February 21, 2002 editions.

This government is bent on destroying our family. You may be aware that my elder brother (Mohammed), heir apparent to the family, is languishing in prison. Therefore, I am soliciting for genuine partners that I can invest the family fortune that is scattered all over the world. According to my estimation in West Africa alone we still have about U.S.$20 million in cash in different security companies that we intend to siphon abroad through your assistance for the purpose of investment in areas of your interest. Contact me as a handsome reward of 10% of the total sum awaits you subject to our negotiation and agreement. You can contact me via e-mail for security reason for further details for now. In the event of you not being interested in this proposal, endeavor to keep this highly confidential!

Thanks and God bless!
Sincerely,
Abba Abacha

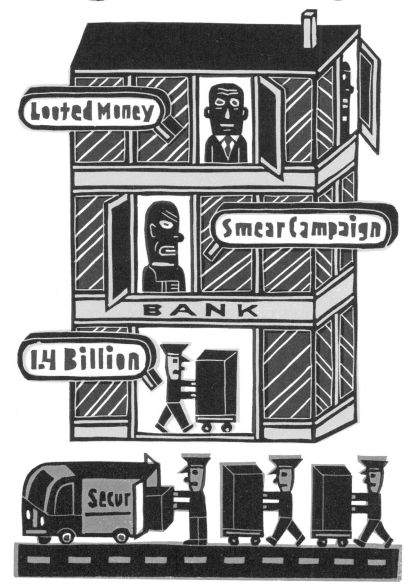

From: Dr. Mrs. Mariam Abacha <mb36nd@yahoo.co.uk>
Date: Tuesday, August 13, 2002, 11:17:06
Subject: assistance

ASSISTANCE

Dear Sir,

I am Dr. Mrs. Mariam Abacha, wife of the late Nigeria head of state, General Sani Abacha who died on the 8th of June 1998 while still on active duty. I am contacting you in view of the fact that we will be of great assistance to each other likeness developing a cordial relationship. I currently have the sum of twenty four million U.S. dollars (U.S.$24,000,000.00) cash in a vault of a certain security company which I intend to use for investment like real estate development in your country. This money came as a payback for the failed debt buy back contract deal between my late husband and some foreigners. I must inform you that the foreigners tried what they felt was good for the deal they had with my late husband and at the end of the present government says it was scam on our country's multi-billion debt to IMF, World Bank and Paris Club.

The partners returned my husband's share of U.S.$24,000,000.00 and lodged in my husband's security company of which I am director until now. The new civilian government have intensified their probe on my husband's finances and business empire.

In view of these, I acted fast to withdraw the U.S.$24,000,000.00 and deposited it in Eurolite Services BV, Amsterdam, The Netherlands. No record ever existed concerning the money traceable by the government. The fund was paid cash. Due to the current situation in the country concerning government attitude towards my family, it has become quite impossible for me to make use of this money within. Let me refer you to this web site and get more details about my family, funds being recovered and how we are being subjected to different treatments to the name of searching for looted funds (http://www.guardian.co.uk/business/story/0,3604,563533,00.html). The present government in Nigeria had frozen and seized all my bank accounts both here in Nigeria and abroad. Thus on your consent to proceed in the business I expect you to contact me urgently.

Bearing in mind that your assistance is needed to transfer this fund, I propose a percentage of 20% of the total sum to you for the expected service and assistance, 10% for offsetting expenses incurred in the course of this transaction. Your urgent response is highly needed as to stop further contacts. All correspondence must be by the e-mail address above. I must use this opportunity to implore you to exercise the utmost indulgence to keep this matter extraordinarily confidential whatever your decision is while I await your prompt response.

N.B. Because of the security being mounted on the members of my family, I have decided that this transaction be kept in utmost secrecy, remember to include your private tel/fax or mobile number for easy communication.

Best regards,
Dr. Mrs. Mariam Abacha

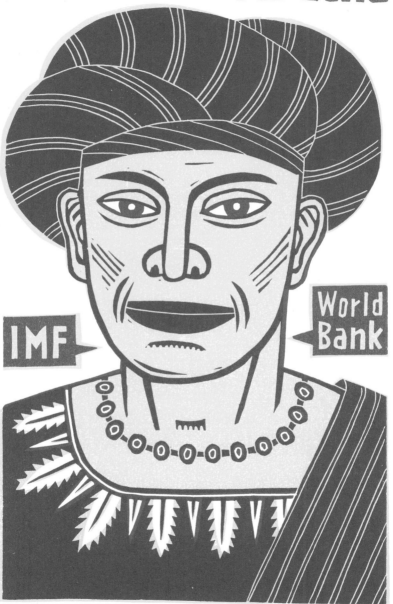

From: Isabella Ikeh <princessiseykeh1@hotmail.com>
Date: Wednesday, November 20, 2002, 02:37:32
Subject: urgent

URGENT

I know that this mail will come to you as a surprise but due to the importance of this situation, I need your help to my mother and sister.

I am Princess Isabella Ikeh, daughter of Chief Oti Onyekwere, the king of Ogoni Kingdom. I am 25 years old and a graduate of mass communication. My father was the king of Ogoni Kingdom, the highest oil producing area in Nigeria. He was in charge of reviving royalties from the multi-national oil companies and government on behalf of the oil producing communities in Nigeria.

After the hanging of the Ogoni Nine(9) including Ken Saro Wiwa by the late dictator General Sani Abacha, my father suffered stroke and died December 27th last year. But before his death, he called me and told me he has twenty three million five hundred and sixty thousand dollars (U.S.$23,560,000.00) cash in his possession, specially deposited in a security vault company here.

He advised me not to tell anybody except my mother who is the last wife of the eight(8) wives that he married. My mother did not bear any male child for him. Which implies that all my fathers properties, companies etc., we have no share in them because my mother has no male child according to African tradition.

My father therefore secretly gave me all the relevant documents of the said money, and told me that I should use this money with my mother and my younger sisters because he knows that traditionally, if he dies, we cannot get anything as inheritance.

He importantly advised me that I should seek foreign assistance and that I should not invest this money here in Nigeria because of his other wives and male children who happen to be my elders. I am soliciting for your immediate assistance to get a bungalow for us, where I will live with my mother and two younger sisters and further advise where and how I will invest the balance money overseas, possibly on products of your company and other profitable ventures.

I believe that by the special grace of God, you will help us move this money out of Nigeria to any country of your choice where we can invest this money judiciously with you. You are entitled to a reasonable part of this money based on our agreement, and God will bless you as you help us.

Please reply through my e-mail. Looking forward to hear from you as soon as possible.

Remain blessed,
Isabella Ikeh

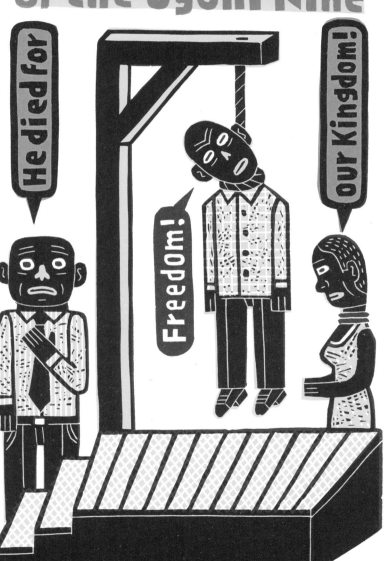

From: John Henry <wisdom_012003@yahoo.com>
Date: Friday, December 13, 2002, 11:36:52
Subject: kingdom investment!

KINGDOM INVESTMENT

Beloved in Christ,

it is a privilege to write to you and to relate my testimony. I was a Moslem and a retired military top officer in the Nigerian army that served under the past military regime. I was the financial secretary to the Armed Force Ruling Council (AFRC). With my position as a financial secretary, I was able to divert up to U.S.$45,000,000.00 (U.S.$ forty five million) into my personal bank account, hoping to invest the money when I'm retired.

Immediately I got retired, I was converted from Moslem to Christian when I was preached about the words of God through my cousin Pastor Paul Osakwe. I then gave my life to Christ and became a Born Again Christian.

Since I gave my life to Christ, I had no rest of mind. Sometimes I think of the souls I killed when I was a soldier and the dubious ways I diverted my country's money into my personal bank account. I then decided to seek the face of God for forgiveness and after fasting and praying, through divine revelation, the Almighty God revealed to me that the only way I could have rest of mind is when I use all my money to do the work of God. I immediately disclosed my revelation to my pastor and he was happy with me.

I have been thinking of the particular thing to do for my God before this present civilian president of my country set up a panel (Honourable Oputa Panel) to probe the bank account of the past military officers like me. Instead of loosing this money to my government, I quickly withdrew my money out of my account and deposited the money in a finance and security company for safety.

My pastor has advised me to sneak out of the country with the money to sow it into a ministry abroad. I have decided to sow this money into your ministry. I am making arrangement to come over to your country but you need to receive this money from the finance and security company in cash before I come over.

The cash has been packaged by the security company in consignments and ready for shipment but the security company requires the address of the receiver. Please send to me your names, address and your telefax number where I can fax the airway bill to you for claim of the consignment over there.

I look forward to your response.
God bless you,
Deacon John Henry

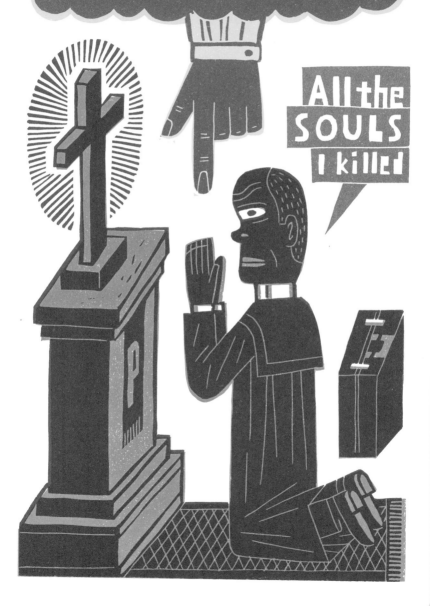

From: aminu005 aminu <aaminu005@caramail.com>
Date: Tuesday, December 10, 2002, 03:29
Subject: strictly confidential (proposal)

Strictly Confidential

Dear Sir,

I am Dr. Robinson Taju Onyeruegbulem, the twin brother of Group Captain Anthony Onyeruegbulem, the past military governor of Edo State in the Federal Republic of Nigeria. He was the governor who handed over power to the present governor, Chief Lucky N. Igbinedion on May 29th, 2000.

Unfortunately he died two months ago in a hotel in Kaduna, when he went for the ANPP (All Nigeria Peoples Party) National Convention held at Abuja. The burial has just been shifted to December this year, his body has been deposited in a mortuary in Abuja.

But there is a certain amount he deposited in my name with a security company during his tenure as military governor of Edo State. That money I want to transfer to Amsterdam onward delivery to an account in your country. I hope to invest 50% of the total sum in your country after the deal has been completed. All I need is a God fearing person, trustworthy and who will not betray trust.

I am ready to part with your percentage charges between you and my lawyer. The total sum is U.S.$81 million. This letter must be treated as a top secret since I am still serving with the present government as a resident doctor at Central Hospital Lagos, Nigeria. All I want is your assistance by providing me with your phone and fax numbers so that we can discuss.

Waiting to hear from you.

Yours faithfully,
Dr. Robinson Taju Onyeruegbulem
234-1-7754093 (private)
234-803-3206813 (mobile)
fax 234-1-7599055

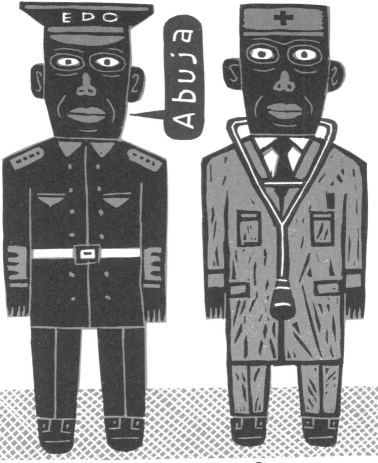

From: Dr. Homa Pola <hom_pola@fsmail.net>
Date: Monday, February 2, 2004, 18:23:37
Subject: very urgent

VERY URGENT

From the desk of Dr. Homa Pola
E-mail address (Homa_pola2004@yahoo.com)

Attn. Sir

My name is Dr. Homa Pola, the manager credit and foreign bills of Union Bank Plc. I am writing in respect of a foreign customer of my bank with account number 14-255-2004/utb/t who perished in a plane crash (Korean Air Flight 801) on August 6, 1997 next to Won Pat International Airport, Guam. 228 passengers lost their lives.

Since the demise of this our customer, I personally have watched with keen interest to see the next of kin but all has proved abortive as no one has come to claim his funds of U.S.$20.5 million (twenty million five hundred thousand united states dollars), which has been with my branch for a very long time. On this note, I decided to seek for whom his name shall be used as the next of kin as no one has come up to be the next of kin. The banking ethics here does not allow such money to stay more than seven years, because money will be recalled to the bank treasury as unclaimed after this period. In view of this I got your contact through a trade journal after realizing that your name and country is similar to the deceased. I will give you 25% of the total.

Upon the receipt of your response, I will send you by fax or e-mail the application, bank's fax number and the next step to take.

I will not fail to bring to your notice that this business is hitch free and that you should not entertain any fear as all modalities for fund transfer can be finalized within five banking days, after you apply to the bank as a relation to the deceased. When you receive this letter kindly send me an e-mail signifying your decision including your private tel/fax numbers for quick communication.

Respectfully submitted,
Dr. Homa Pola

KAL Flight 801

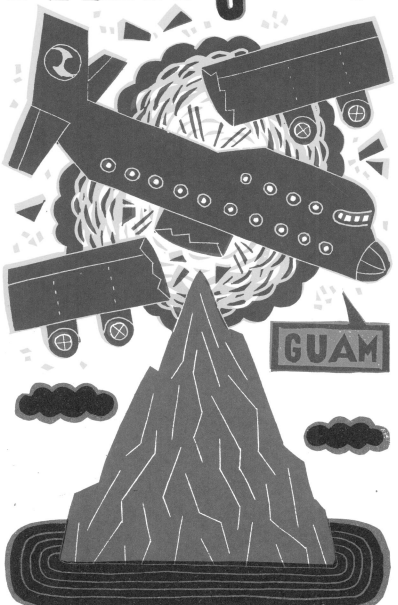

GUAM

From: Professor Frank Obi <professorfranko@netscape.com>
Date: Sunday, March, 2003, 23:33:06
Subject: sincere proposition

ATTENTION: MD/CEO

I am Professor Frank Obi, a solicitor at law and a partner at P. O. Williams and Co. I am the attorney to Mr. James McCullough, an expatriate, who used to work with Shell Development Company in Nigeria.

On the 21st of April 1999, my client, his wife and their children were involved in a car accident along Sagbama Express Road. All occupants of the vehicle lost their lives. Since then, I have made enquiries to several embassy's and home offices, to locate any of my client's extended relatives, but this has proved unsuccessful.

I contact you to assist in expatriating the estate left behind by my client before the estate reverts to the government or his cash accounts declared unserviceable by the bank where the deposit is lodged.

Particularly, the Standard Security, where the deceased had an account valued at about 38.6 million dollars, has issued me, being the executor of the estate, a notice to provide the next of kin or have the account unserviceable, to carry out due process on the deposit within the next twenty-one working days.

Since I have been unsuccessful in locating any relatives in the past 2 years since his demise, I seek your consent to present you as the next of kin of the deceased to claim the deposit (plus interest) currently with Standard Security. As executor of the estate, I will be legally and fully involved in the claims process, and therefore in a position to guide you through the processes as contained in the laws of our land.

I have all relevant documents to wit. All what is required is your honest co-operation to enable us successfully conclude this project. I guarantee that this will be executed under and within the dictates of the laws of the land as regards to inheritance claims. Consequently you will be protected from any breaches of these laws.

I have left the discussion and agreement for your re-numeration for your involvement until you confirm your interest and readiness to assist me in this project. Please get in touch with me via my e-mail address to enable us discuss further.

Regards,
Professor Frank Obi (Esq)
Telephone: 234-1-776-0962
Fax: 234-1-759-4725

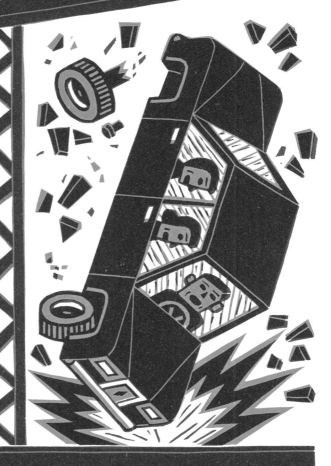

From: Adryn <michael@levele.com>
Date: Wednesday, August 20, 2003, 19:43:52
Subject: confidential business proposition

CONFIDENTIAL PROPOSITION

Dear Friend,

I am Mr. Michael Obong, credit officer of Gulf Bank of Nigeria Plc. Onitsha Branch. I have an urgent and very confidential business proposition for you.

On June 6, 1999, a Canadian oil consultant with the Exxon Mobil Oil of Nigerian Corporation, Mr. Peter Boulter, made a numbered time (fixed) deposit for twelve calendar months, valued at U.S.$18,250,000.00 (eighteen million two hundred and fifty thousand dollars only) in my branch. Upon maturity, I sent a routine notification to his forwarding address but got no reply. After a month, we sent a reminder and finally we discovered from his contract employers, the Exxon Mobil Oil Co. that Mr. Peter Boulter died from an boat mishap in the Niger delta. On further investigation, I found out that he died without making a will and all attempts to trace his next of kin were fruitless. Mr. Peter Boulter did not declare any kin or relations in all his official documents.

This sum of U.S.$18,250,000.00 is still sitting in my bank and the interest is being rolled over with the principal sum at the end of each year. No one will ever come forward to claim it. According to laws here in Nigeria, at the expiration of 5 (five) years, the money will revert to the ownership of the Nigerian government if nobody applies to claim the fund.

Consequently, my proposal is that I will like you as a foreigner to stand in as the next of kin to Mr. Peter Boulter so that the fruits of this old man's labor will not get into the hands of some corrupt government officials. This is simple. I will like you to provide immediately your full name and address so that the attorney will prepare the necessary documents and affidavits that will put you in place as the next of kin. We shall employ the services of an attorney for drafting and notarization of the will and to obtain the necessary documents and letter of probate/administration in your favor for the transfer. A bank account in any part of the world that you will provide will then facilitate the transfer of this money to you as the beneficiary/next of kin.

The money will be paid into your account for us to share in the ratio of 65% for me and 30% for you and 5% for expenses incurred in the course of the transaction. There is no risk at all as all the paperwork for this transaction will be done by the attorney and with my position as the credit officer guarantees the successful execution of this transaction. If you are interested, please reply immediately to my e-mail box.

Upon your response, I shall then provide you with more details and relevant documents that will help you understand the transaction. You should observe utmost confidentiality and rest assured that this transaction would be most profitable for both of us. Awaiting your urgent reply,

Mr. Michael Obong

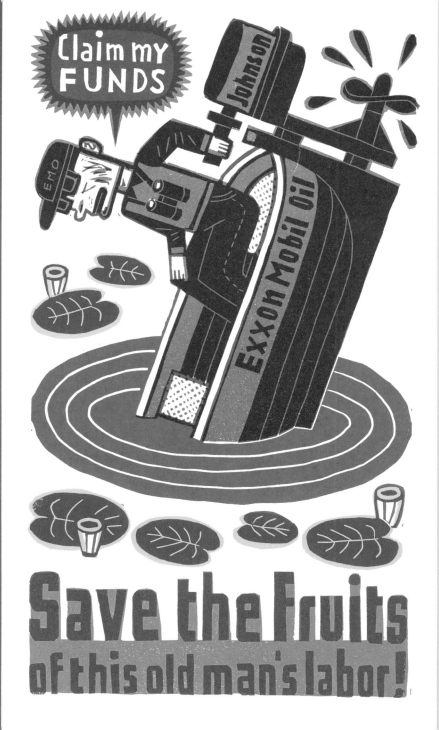

From: Doctor Kamala <doctor_kamala@voila.fr>
Date: Friday, March 14, 2003, 11:24:06
Subject: hello

HELLO

Dear Friend,

I am Dr. Anthony Kamala. I am a medical doctor, a Kenyan man by nationality, but I work here in Nigeria as a specialist medical doctor to the governor of Lagos State, Nigeria. I am the Senior Doctor of (G.S.H.O.N.) the Government Specialist Hospital of Nigeria.

I have a case of a man who had an accident and was rushed to the hospital by some good samaritans. Myself and some other specialist doctors working under me tried all we could, but unfortunately the man died. Before he died I discovered a small box with him, I opened the box and found so many documents in it. I then realized that he is a German man who only came into Nigeria for business, but unfortunately he died.

The other documents inside his box are documents which he used in depositing the sum of U.S.$18 million dollars with a security company here in Nigeria, including the picture of the money box which was used to be deposited with the diplomatic security company. Unfortunately he died and left all these.

I have tried all I could to reach any of his family members, but I couldn't get anyone from his family. He is single and not married, so his status really made it difficult for me to get any of his relatives.

With my position as specialist doctor to the governor and as the Senior Doctor of the (G.S.H.O.N.) Government Specialist Hospital of Nigeria I won't be able to act as the next of kin to the consignment and clear the consignment (the fund).

This is why I hereby solicit your assistance to act as the next of kin in the collection of this fund from the security company. I shall provide you with the necessary documents for the collection of the fund. If you can assist in this transaction, I shall give you 15% of the fund as your share and for your assistance in this transaction. 80% of the fund shall be mine, and we (you and me) shall both invest the remaining 5% for the settlement of any expenditure that has been made during this transaction.

If you are interested and can assist, please reply immediately, so that we can move forward in this transaction. Please it is very, very confidential.

Best regards,
Dr. Anthony Kamala

N.B. Please do reply to my private e-mail address: dr_kamala@myself.com

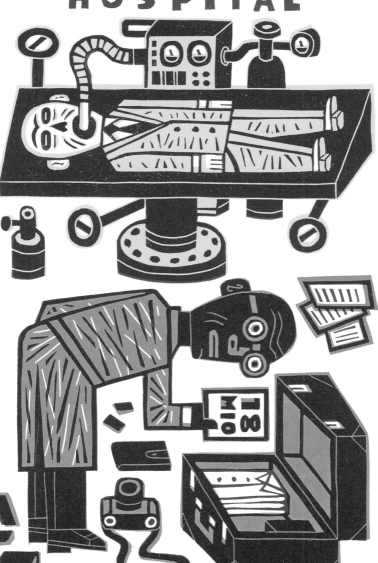

G.S.H.O.N.

HOSPITAL

From: Patrick Kofi <patrick4000@ecplaza.net>
Date: Thuesday, March 27, 2003, 02:55:59
Subject: reply needed

STRICTLY CONFIDENTIAL

We are members of a special committee for budget and planning of the Nigerian National Petroleum Corporation (NNPC). This committee is principally concerned with contract awards and approval. With our positions, we have successfully secured for ourselves the sum of thirty one million five hundred thousand United States dollars (U.S.$31.5 million). This amount was carefully manipulated by over-invoicing of an old contract.

Based on information gathered about you, we believe you would be in a position to help us in transferring this fund (U.S.$31.5 million) into a safe account. It has been agreed that the owner of the account will be compensated with 30% of the remitted funds, while we keep 60% as the initiators and 10% will be set aside to offset expenses and pay the necessary taxes.

All modalities of this transaction have been carefully worked out and once started it will not take more than seven (7) working days, with your full support. This transaction is 100% risk free. Be rest assured of success.

If this proposal satisfies you, please reach us only by e-mail for more information. Please, treat this as urgent and very important.

Yours faithfully,
Dr. Patrick Kofi

100% RISK FREE

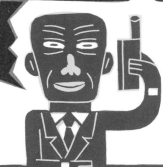 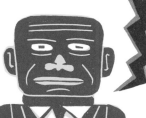

carefully **manipulated**

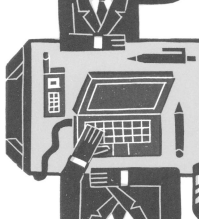 

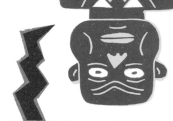 

by **overinvoicing.**

From: Dr. Ken Amobi <drken@post.cz>
Date: Tuesday, May 13, 2003, 13:43:46
Subject: business proposal

TRUST IS OUR BEACON

My Dear,
we wish to solicit your assistance to provide us with a solution to a money transfer. We are members of the Special Committee newly instituted in my country. Our duty is to review all contracts awarded to foreign firms and contractors.

It may interest you to know that most of the contracts awarded were over invoiced or inflated. One of such contracts has been identified. The said contract was originally executed by an Italian based firm (Straberg Italiano Spa) in 1996, to supply 250,000 monax turbine polypropylene plant sand 150,000 bpsd for a refinery and pipeline reconstruction and computer optimization for plants "A" to another refinery as part of the measure taken to aid the turn around maintenance to recoup the almost collapsed refineries in my country. The total amount approved by then for this project was put at U.S.$125,000,000.00.

The actual amount used for executing the contract was estimated to be U.S.$ 86,000,000.00, which has since been paid to the foreign contractor. The remaining sum of U.S.$ 39,000.000.00 was inflated. The over inflated amount is lying in one of the country's apex bank escrow accounts, waiting to be dispatched to a designated bank account. More information shall be made known to you upon the positive confirmation from your good self that you are willing to assist us in the completion of the understated proposal. What we want from you now is to provide a safe account where the inflated amount will be transferred. We also need the name of your choice company, address and tel/fax numbers.

By doing so, your company will be created as artificial contractor and thus can lay claim to the inflated amount. My colleagues and I have agreed to compensate the owner of the account with 10% of the total amount remitted. We shall keep 80% and 10% will be reserved for taxes and other miscellaneous expenses. We intend to consummate this transaction within the shortest possible time based on your cooperation and support.

The chance of success is sure and besides, we have the support of colleagues from other renowned government departments. Our chances of success are as good as gold. This project demands mutual support, commitment and trust. Therefore, we desire consistent and purposeful participation as we thread the part of greatness. Mutual trust is our beacon.

Endeavor to remain in steady contact and send me your personal phone and fax numbers for easier communication and further clarification. I honestly assure you that this transaction is 100% risk-free.

Best regards,
Dr. Ken Amobi

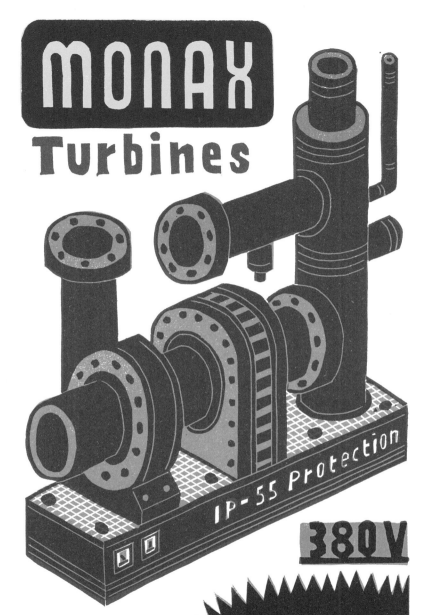

From: Dr. Bill Akulunon <fmysc@indiatimes.com>
Date: Saturday, October 12, 2002, 20:16:30
Subject: All African Games

8TH ALL AFRICAN GAMES

Dear Sir,

I am Dr. Bill Akulunon, the accountant of the Federal Ministry of Youths, Sports and Culture—parent body of the Local Organizing Committee of the 8th All African Games tagged »COJA 2003« being held in my country next year. In the course of our preparation, a huge sum of money running into millions of United States dollars was budgeted by the present civilian administration of our President Chief Olusegun Obasanjo for the successful prosecution of this competition. In the same vein, the Supreme Council for Sport in Africa also made millions of dollars available for the competition. However, in my capacity as chief accountant of both Local Organizing Committee (LOC) and the Federal Ministry of Youth, Sports and Culture, my colleagues and I in sensitive positions were able to influence the award of the contract for the supply and installation of some of the equipment that will be used for the competition.

The contractor agreed to give us 10% of the total contract sum, if we were able to influence the contract in their favour. Other foreign firms bided for this same contract, but we were able to influence the board to award the contract to the firm we had this agreement with. This contract has been successfully executed and they have been paid 90% of their total contract sum, remaining the balance of 10% which we never wanted them to collect on our behalf because of the fear that they might not fulfil their promise. It is pertinent to note that the remaining balance of seven million United States dollars (US$7,000,000.00) is lying in the suspense account of the First Chartered Bank Lagos, ready for transfer into an oversea account.

I have been unanimously mandated to seek for an honest and trustworthy foreign partner who will assist in ensuring the successful transfer of the above sum of money into his personal account, since the Nigerian Code of Conduct Bureau does not permit us to operate a foreign account as public servants. On the successful remittance of the fund (US$7,000,000.00) into your nominated account, for your kind assistance you will be adequately compensated.

Be assured that the modalities and logistics towards the successful transfer of this fund have been worked out. We kindly request that you accord it the highest level of secrecy it deserves. Note that, this transaction is legal and free from all sorts of risk and trouble. It does not contravene the laws of my country nor any international laws, hence the whole approval for the transfer will be official and legally processed. This transaction will be concluded within five (5) working days if we follow it up and give the serious attention it deserves.

Awaiting your prompt response,
Dr. Bill Akulunon

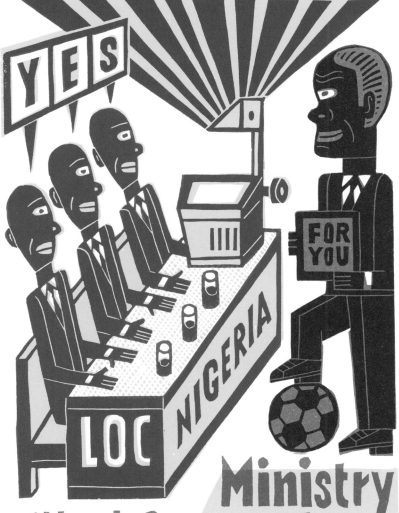

From: Usman Ali <usman_a99@juno.com>
Date: Saturday, March 15, 2003, 12:25:06
Subject: in trust

IN TRUST

Attn. Sir,

I am Mr. Usman Ali, former special adviser on petroleum and economic matters to the late Head of State of the Federal Republic of Nigeria, General Sani Abacha. Because of my strategic position in the former government and also being a close confidant of the Head of State, I was able to acquire personally the sum of U.S.$ 20,000,000.00 (twenty million United States dollars) presently lodged in Union Bank of Nigeria Plc.

I made this money largely through consultation fees and good faith fees paid by foreign oil companies prior to allocation of deep water oil blocks and other lifting/prospecting rights. Nigeria is the 6th largest producer/exporter of crude petroleum in the world.

As you are probably aware, Nigeria is prone to political/economic instability and hyper inflation. I have therefore resolved to invest my money abroad, preferable in real estate properties and importation of goods for safety and optimum returns on investments. However, straight transfer of this money into a bank abroad will present two major problems:

1. The tax incidence will be too high, as much as 60% of this money will go up in taxes, levies, penalties etc.

2. As an ex serviceman in a former military government on which the present democratic government of Chief Olusegun Obasanjo is fighting very hard to freeze the accounts of the men that served in the government of General Abacha.

As a result, the government deliberate restricted the flight of capital abroad. The solution is to courier this money in cash abroad, through a courier service company here in Nigeria in conjunction with the embassy in Nigeria. The money will be packed in a diplomatic bag or carton tagged »diplomatic luggage« which will be addressed to you. This system is secret and the money is therefore untraceable. It is the system used by most top government officials in Nigeria to remove their fortunes to safety abroad.

All I now need is a honest partner who can receive the money on my behalf. There is absolutely no risk involved in this transaction as the money will be delivered to you in United States dollar bills.

If you are interested in assisting me, please send to me by e-mail immediately your preferred contact address where this money should be delivered to you. For your help and assistance in this deal, you will receive 30% of this money in cash, 10% will be set aside to offset all expenses while the remaining 60% is for me. Finally, please urgently e-mail your personal phone and fax numbers for an easy communication. Expecting to hear from you,

Best regards,
Mr. Usman Ali

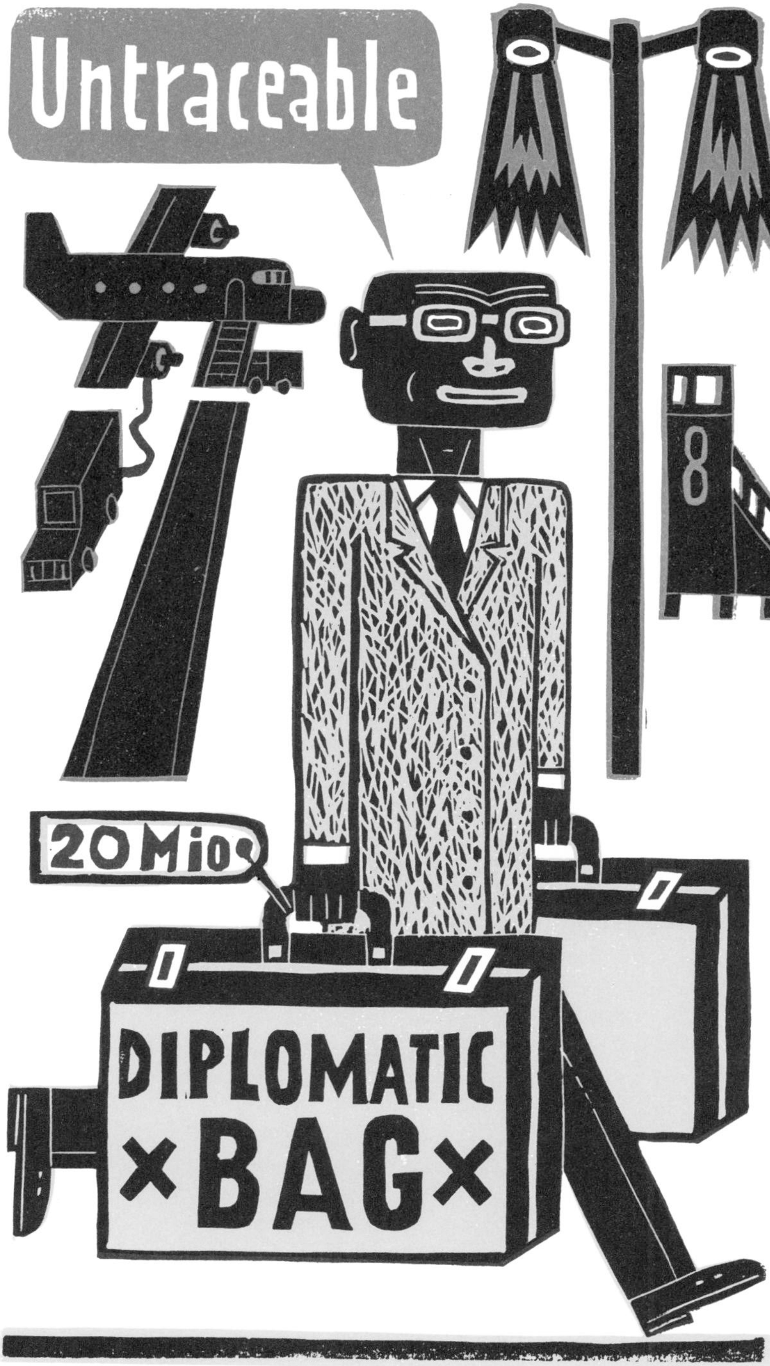
Untraceable
20 Mio
8
DIPLOMATIC
×BAG×

From: Adamu Yazid <adamu_yazid@yahoo.com>
Date: Tuesday, August 7, 2001, 08:27:11
Subject: trust and confidence

CASH AND NOT FAKE

#101 Annamdi Azikiwe Crescent, Tunibu Square
Lagos, Nigeria
Tel. 234-1-7591531
Fax 234-1-7590922

I am chairman of the audit committee in the Central Bank of Nigeria, set up by the present democratic government of Nigeria. I came across your particulars through a business journal. I will be obliged to have an eventful and worthy business deal with you.

So far, I have in my possession one hundred and fifty million genuine U.S. dollars physical cash and not fake. Of course, the dollars were intentionally stained to avoid spendable by any sighted hawk or interception group or person before getting to me. The source is not questionable and there is no legal infringement whatsoever. More so, I have now the ready source of the chemical in the USA to clean the stained dollars which has been my initial problem.

If you indicate your interest to do this business with me, I will use my influence as chairman of the audit committee to transfer this money to Global Security House in Sweden for safe keeping.

All I require you to do is assist me in claiming the money. If you show interest I will give you the documents which you will use to claim the money in Sweden. I need your good advice on a remunerative venture in your country which I will like to invest some of this money. Note 40% accrues to you as the owner of the nominated foreign bank account were this money will be paid to.

Thanks from
Adamu Yazid

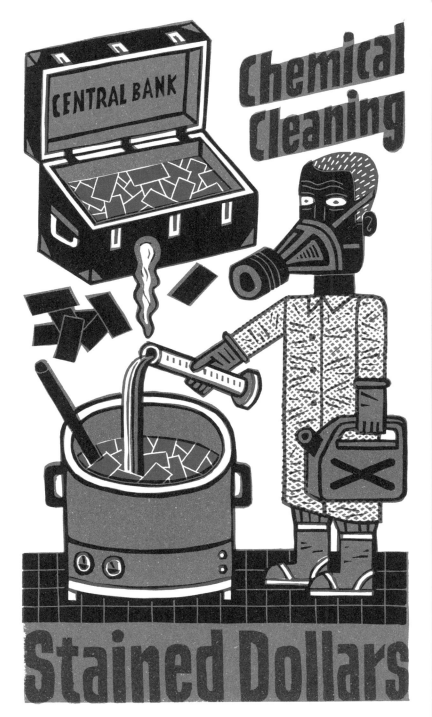

Chemical Cleaning

Stained Dollars

From: Shepherd Allah <shepherd4@latinmail.com>
Date: Wednesday, February 11, 2004, 02:23:04
Subject: investment

From: Mrs. Halima Mahmoud

Attn. Sir/Madam,

I am an investor from Iraq, currently in the Republic of Benin because of the civil war in my country. I wish to invest in a country with political stability, reliable, dependable infrastructure and security of life and property. A friend who is a foreigner on a working visit in Cotonou, the capital of Benin, gave me your contact address. She said that you may be willing to assist me in my investment plans if I am lucky.

It may interest you to know that I am ready and willing to invest the sum of 13.5 million U.S. dollars into your company or any good and profitable business that you may suggest based on your expertise know how. This amount was willed to my children and me by my late husband. I am willing to invest in a company with potentials for growth and stability, if your company by law allows a foreign investor.

I will be very happy if this enquiry receives urgent attention. You should mail your acceptance by sending to me your personal and company profile as I will also send to you all required information about myself and the help that I need from you about my investment plans.

Hoping for a very successful business relationship with you.
Best regards,
Mrs. Halima Mahmoud.

N.B. You should reply me on this particular mailbox: mhalima@sify.com, because it is purposely for this transaction. Thanks for your understanding.

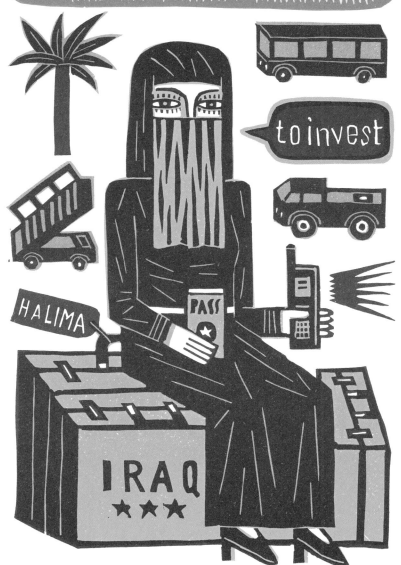

From: Mrs. Mobutu Sese-Seko <mm_seseseko2003@yahoo.co.in>
Date: Saturday, November 15, 2003, 13:37:16
Subject: important information

IMPORTANT INFORMATION

Dear friend,

I am Mrs. Sese-Seko, widow of late president Mobutu Sese-Seko of Zaire, now known as Democratic Republic of Congo (DRC). I am moved to write you this letter in confidence considering my present circumstance and situation.

I escaped along with my husband and two of our sons, Kongolo and Nzanga, out of Democratic Republic of Congo (DRC) to Abidjan, Côte d'Ivoire. Later my family and I moved to Morocco where my husband died of cancer disease. However, due to this situation we decided to change most of my husband's billions of dollars deposited in a Swiss bank and other countries into other forms of money coded for safe purpose, because the new head of state (Dr.) Mr. Laurent Kabila has made arrangement with the Swiss government and other European countries to freeze all my late husband's treasures deposited in some European countries.

Hence my children and I decided laying low in Africa to study the situation till when things gets better, like now that president Kabila is dead and the son taking over (Joseph Kabila). One of my late husband's chateaux in southern France was confiscated by the French government and as such I had to change my identity that my investment will not be traced and confiscated.

I have deposited the sum of twenty five million United States dollars (U.S.$25,000,000.00) with a security company for safekeeping. The funds are security coded to prevent them from knowing the content. What I want you to do is to indicate your interest that you will assist us by receiving the money on our behalf. Acknowledge this message, so that I can introduce you to my son (Kongolo) who has the out modalities for the claim of the said funds. I want you to assist in investing this money, but I will not want my identity revealed. I will also want to buy properties and stocks in multi-national companies and to engage in other safe and non-speculative investments.

May I at this point emphasize the high level of confidentiality which this business demands and hope you will not betray the trust and confidence which I repose in you. In conclusion, if you want to assist us, my son shall put you in the picture of the business, tell you where the funds are currently being maintained and also discuss other modalities including remuneration for your services.

For this reason kindly furnish us your contact information, that is your personal telephone and fax number for confidential purpose and acknowledge receipt of this mail using the above e-mail address.

Best regards,
Mrs. M. Mobutu Sese-Seko
Reply to: mmseseseko2003@yahoo.ie

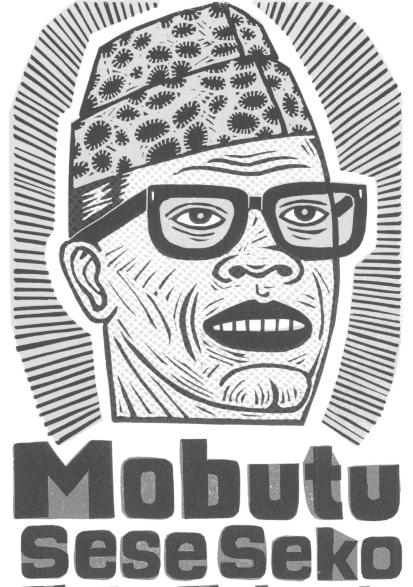

Mobutu Sese Seko Kuku Ngbendu Wa Za Banga

From: Edward Mambo <edmab24@yahoo.com>
Date: Thuesday, October 11, 2001, 06:18:59
Subject: offer for help

OFFER FOR HELP

Sir,

May I briefly introduce myself. I am Edward Mambo of the Democratic Republic of Congo (formerly Zaire) and the former aide de camp of the late President Laurent Kabila of blessed memory.

I am presently living in Nigeria on asylum. In case you are wondering, I got your contact from the foreign trade office of the Nigeria Chamber of Commerce and Industry. The events of the past one year in my country has been very unfortunate. The late President Kabila successfully toppled the very corrupt government of the late dictator Mobutu Sese Seko and ruled justly and peacefully for a few months. Unfortunately, the Tutsi from Goma, the northern part of the country rebelled against his government and since then my country has been at war.

I am very dedicated and committed to winning the war against the rebels until recently when to my shock I found out that senior army officers and government officials were stealing public funds, looting government treasury and sending them to foreign countries. They have exploited the war situation to bring back the lawlessness and corruption of the Mobutu days.

After the late President Kabila was assassinated under very questionable circumstances, I knew I was in danger of losing from both ends. Due to this development and as a way of survival, I have joined the train. I have in my possession funds amounting to U.S.$15.5 million. In the usual manner of conveying such funds, the money is in defaced form in a trunk box for security reasons. It is now in the safe custody of a security company.

My problem is that the financial law of Nigeria does not give asylum seekers any financial rights. And because of the economic instability and religious crisis, I have decided that it will be unwise to attempt investing the funds here. The climate here is very unfavorable and as a result, I have not disclosed even to my hosts anything about this fund.

Now I am seeking foreign assistance to transfer the funds overseas. If you can assist, I am willing to give you 20% of the funds, that is U.S.$3.1 million. You will understand that my entire life and future depend on this money and I shall be very grateful if you can assist me. The major thing I demand from you is the absolute assurance that the money will be safe and you will not sit on it when it is transferred to your account.

If you are ready to be of assistance, please contact me immediately, so that I can furnish you with the modalities for the transaction and what is expected of you. I shall be most grateful if you maintain utmost confidentiality and keep this message entirely to yourself.

Best regards,
Mr. Edward Mambo

LAURENT KABILA

May his Soul rest in peace!

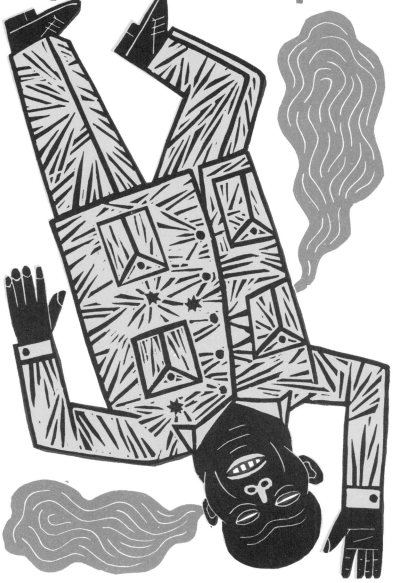

From: Emmanuel Kabila <emmakabila4eva@tatanova.com>
Date: Tuesday, January 20, 2004, 10:27:21
Subject: investment offer

FAMILY BUSINESS OFFER

Dear,

this letter might surprise you, because we have not met neither in person nor by correspondence. But I believe one day you get to know somebody either in physical or through correspondence. I got your contact through some discreet inquiry from the Chamber of Commerce and Industry. One has no doubt in your ability to handle a financial business transaction. However, I wish to introduce myself, I am Emmanuel Kishali Kabila, the son of the late Democratic Republic of Congo President Laurent Desiré Kabila of the blessed memory. I write this letter in respect of my intention to invest the sum of U.S.$28 million (twenty eight million United States dollars) with you. I inherited this money from my mother. This money was got through the smuggling and sale of diamond and timber when my father was the head of state. My mother, though not his legal wife, used her privilege position to engage in the business of diamond and timber since she knows that her survival will depend on how much she can get out of the privilege situation.

My father was assassinated on 16th Jan. 01 by one of his bodyguards Lt. Rashidi Kasereke through the conspiracy of some top army officers that wanted to topple him. I escaped because of the fear that I might be arrested by my half brother Lt. General Joseph Kabila, the present head of state. Actually his mother and my mother are not in the best relationship because of the who among them will be the first lady tussle. This ultimately affected their children.

My mother advised me to leave for South Africa, while the funds were deposited with a security company in Madrid, Spain. Honestly I contacted you because I don't want to invest this money in South Africa due to my status here as a political refugee. And moreover I wouldn't want to take risk because this money is all we depend on because my half brother has seized all my father's assets and left me and my mother empty handed. That is why I decided that investing this money abroad should be the best for me. I will be honored if I can be given the privilege of investing this money with your help.

In view of this plight, I expect you to be trustworthy and kind enough to respond to this distress call to save my mother and me from a hopeless future. I hereby agree to compensate your sincere and candid effort in this regard with 20% of the total money and annual 5% of the after tax returns on investment for the first three years. The remaining 75% will be invested meaningfully for our future if possible in your area of business and deterrents sectors of the economy in your country which are dividends yielding. Whatever your decision is please reach me immediately through my private phone or e-mail and keep this letter tight secret for the interest of my family.

Best regards,
Emmanuel Kishali Kabila (for the family)

SMUGGLE

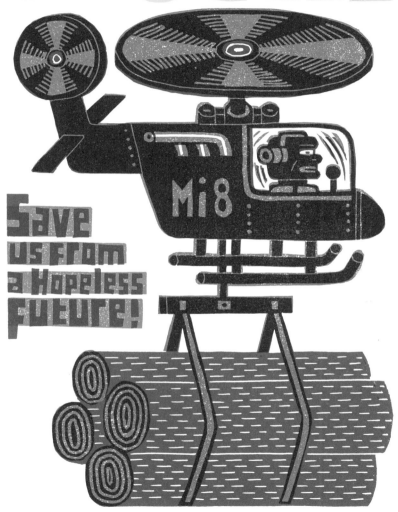

Save us from a Hopeless Future!

Mi 8

Diamonds + Timber

From: Mrs. Sandra Nzama <jameszuma13@hotmail.com>
Date: Thursday, November 18, 2003, 20:12:40
Subject: congratulations!

CONGRATULATIONS FOR YOUR WINNING!

Euro Afro American Lottery Promotion Switzerland
From the desk of Mrs. Sandra Nzama

Dear Sir/Madam,
we happily announce to you the draw of South African 2010 World Cup Bid Lottery Award International, held in Zurich, Switzerland. Your e-mail address attached to ticket number: B9665 75604546 199 with serial number 97560 drew the winning: 60/84/27/17/36, which subsequently won you the lottery award in the 2nd category. Your name has therefore been approved to claim a total sum of U.S.$2,000,000.00 (two million United States dollars) in cash credited to file KPC/9030108308/03. This is from a total cash prize of U.S.$30,000,000.00 (thirty million United States dollars) shared among the first 200 lucky winners in this category world-wide. Please note that your lucky winning number falls within our lottery booklet representative office in South Africa as indicated in the play coupon.

In view of this, your U.S.$2,000,000 (two million United States dollars) would be released through the assistance of our agent in South Africa. He will immediately commence the process to facilitate the release of your funds as soon as you contact him. All participants were selected randomly from world wide web sites through computer draw system and extracted from over 100,000,00 companies and individual e-mail addresses. The lottery program took place to promote South Africa's 2010 World Cup Award.

For security reasons, you are advised to keep your winning information confidential till your claims are processed and your money remitted to you in whatever manner you deem fit to claim your prize. This is part of our precautionary measure to avoid double claiming and unwarranted abuse of this program by some unscrupulous elements. Please you are advised to file for your claim through our agent Mr. James A. Zuma immediately you received this message because you stand a risk of loosing the prize if you fail to claim it within a month from the day you received this notification. His e-mail address is: jameszuma13@hotmail.com, Tel. 27-83-437-4001.

Yours sincerely,
Mrs. Sandra Nzama
(Zonal coordinator)

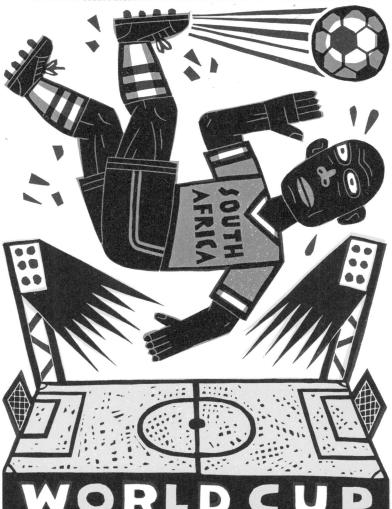

FROM: MR. JONSON JOH

Dear Friend,

I am Mr. Jonson Joh, the only son of the former Director of Finance, Sierra Leone Diamond and Mining Corporation, Dr. Desmond Jonson. I got your contact through a current publication and decided to solicit for your understanding and whole-hearted assistance to receive the sum of U.S.$20.5 million in your bank account and earnest business partnership thereafter.

My name is as above, I am 25 years old, a citizen of Sierra Leone. I lost my parents as a result of the disastrous civil war which lasted for about 12 years in my country. Before the peak of the war, which eventually took my father's life, my father informed me in confidence that he has deposited the above sum in a sus-pense account of a bank in Abidjan, Côte d'Ivoire, where I moved with my younger sister immediately after my father was murdered by the rebels. I now reside here (Abidjan) under political asylum with my 17 years old sister, Precious Jonson.

The money was put in my father's possession by the then government of Alhaji Tejan Kaba for the purchasing of ammunitions to confront the rebels. Now the war in my country is over with the help of ECOMOG soldiers, the present govern-ment of Sierra Leone has revoked the passport of all officers who served under the former regime and now asked countries to expel such persons, at the same time freeze their accounts and confiscate their assets. It is on this note that I am contacting you. I need you to assist me to receive the money into your account by providing me with your bank particulars:

1) Bank name and address
2) Account name and beneficiary
3) Account number and swift code
4) Bank telephone, fax and telex numbers
5) Your private address, telephone and fax numbers

I have in mind to compensate you with 10% of the total money amount, additional 5% for all your expenses incurred in this transaction. I will give you a 20% annual commission in any investment we embark upon in your country. I intend to invest in real estate business, though it depends on how lucrative it is in your country, I also count on your advice and guidance.

Please kindly reach me by a return mail or on the above telephone number to indicate your interest in this business transaction, so as to enable us to discuss this transaction in detail. Finally, I wish to assure you that this transaction is legal and 100% risk free. I have in my possession the legal documents of this deposit. Thanks and God bless as you get back to me as quickly as possible.

Yours sincerely,
Mr. Jonson Joh

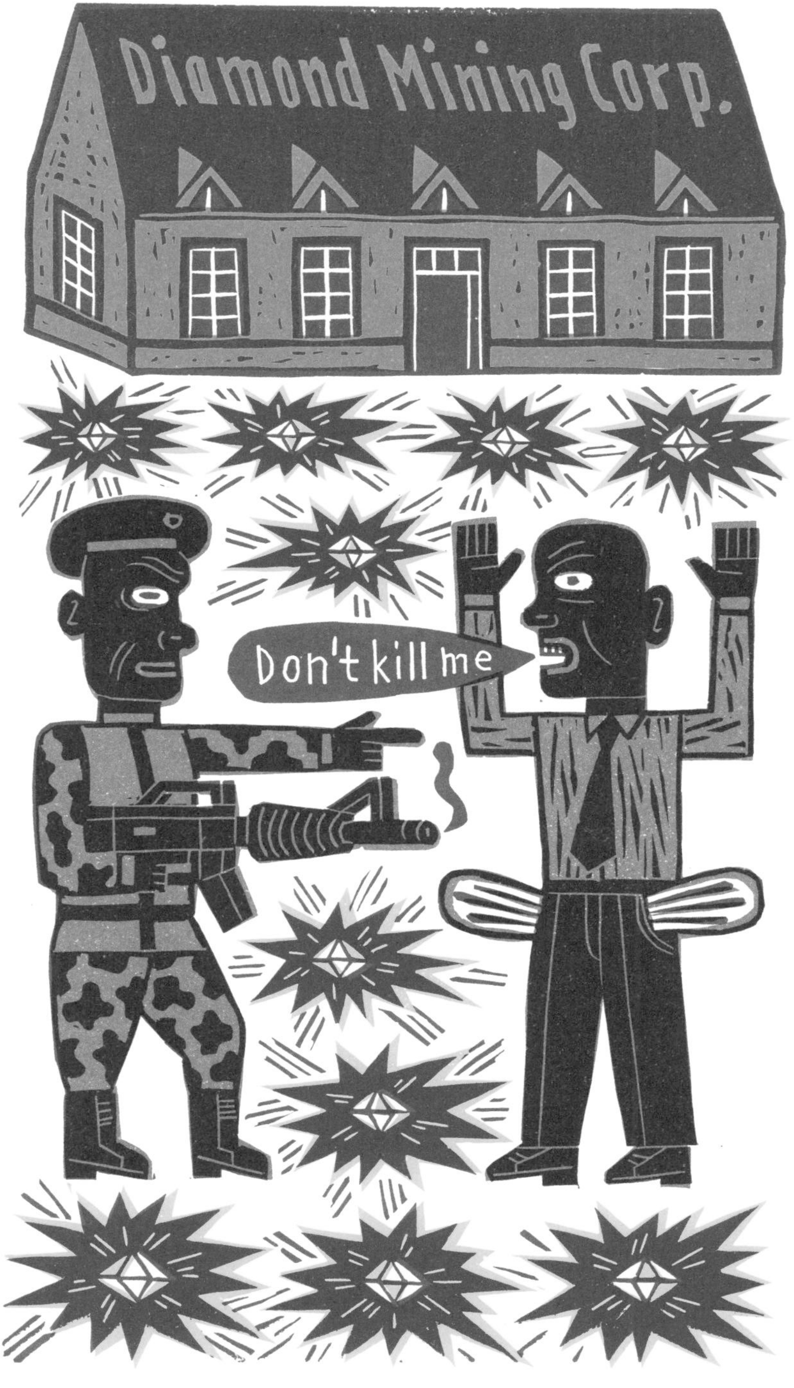
Diamond Mining Corp.
Don't kill me

From: Tatiana Taboh <tatiana.taboh@libero.it>
Date: Friday, November 22, 2002, 10:56:16
Subject: hope of survival

HOPE OF SURVIVAL

Dear Sir,

please I am Tatiana Taboh, the only daughter of late chief Joseph Alfred Taboh from Sierra Leone. I got your contact from the ECOWAS Information Center in Côte d'Ivoire. I am writing you in absolute confidence primarily to seek your assistance to transfer our cash of twenty one million eight hundred thousand dollars ($21,800,000), now in the custody of a bank here in Abidjan, to your private account pending our arrival to your country.

Source of the money: My late father, a native of Mende district in the northern province of Sierra Leone, was the general manager of Sierra Leone Mining Cooperation (S.L.M.C.), Freetown. According to my father, this money was the income from the mining cooperation's over draft and minor sales. Before the peak of the civil war between the rebels forces of major Paul Koroma and the combined forces of ECOMOG peace keeping operation, following the forceful removal from power of the civilian elected president Ahmed Tejan Kabbah, my father had already made arrangements for his family, my mother, my little brother and myself, to be evacuated to Abidjan, Côte d'Ivoire.

My father deposited the fund for the safe custody until after the war when he will join us. During the war and the following indiscriminate looting of public and government properties by the rebel forces, the Sierra Leone Mining Coop. was one of the targets looted and destroyed.

My father including other top government functionaries were attacked and killed by the rebels because of their relationship with the civilian government of Ahmed Tejan Kabbah. My father's death and the news of my uncle's involvement in an airplane crash in January dashed our hope of survival. The untimely deaths caused my mother's heart failure and other related complications so we had to spent a lot of money on her. Now my younger brother and myself are alone in this strange country suffering without any care or help. Without any relation, we are now like refugees and orphans. To this effect, I humbly solicit your assistance in the followings ways:

To assist me claim this fund from the bank as foreign partner/beneficiary, to transfer this money in your name to your country, to make a good arrangement for a joint business investment on our behalf in your country and you, the caretaker, to secure a college for my little brother and myself in your country to further our education and to make arrangement for our travel to your country after you have transferred this fund.

Most importantly, the whole documents issued to my late father after the deposit are all in my custody. I am waiting for your urgent response for a brief discussion and more information. Thanks and God bless you,

Tatiana Taboh and brother Abraham

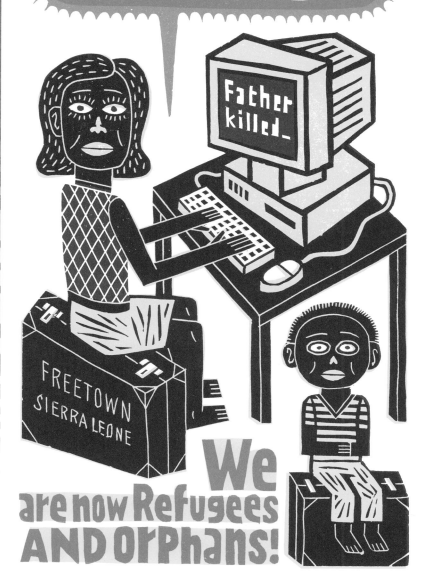

From: Anamb Johana <anambjo@yahoo.com>
Date: Wednesday, September 25, 2002, 10:31:20
Subject: investment proposal

PRIVATE AND URGENT REPLY

Dear Sir/Madam,

I am one of the former advisors on arms control and acquisition to the current president of Sierra Leone, His Excellency Ahmed Kabbah.

Following the civil war in my country, the head of state delegated me to arrange arms purchases from the Netherlands through an independent arm dealer. I was directed for arms worth of thirty six million United States dollars (U.S.$36 million). On arrival in the Netherlands, I defected to the rebels side and declined to go back to Sierra Leone. I decided to divert this fund which was brought through diplomatic means and deposited in a security company here in the Netherlands and declared it to be an official consignment belonging to my foreign affiliate.

Currently, this proposal is to inform you that I want to transfer this fund into any of your personal accounts or company's accounts within the shortest possible time for self keeping. Please note that this transaction demands the highest degree of trust and confidentiality between us, moreover, it's risk free in the sense that I have taken proper care of all formalities regarding it.

In appreciation of your assistance, I have worked out the sharing ratio for this transaction as follows: 70% for my investment in your country under your close supervision and directions, 25% for your effort (help and assistance) and we shall set aside 5% for all incidental expenses.

Please reply on the above e-mail as to give me your private telephone and fax number for confidential communication . As I wait to hear from you, be informed that all communication on this transaction shall be confidential.

Thanks for your anticipated cooperation.
Best regards,
Jim Kaa (0031 613444976)

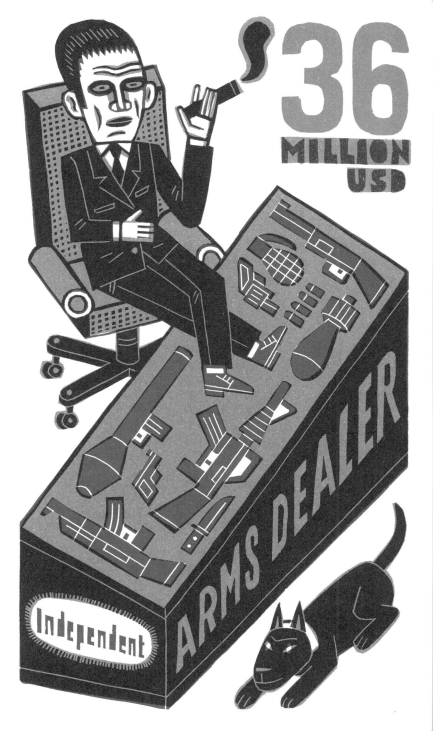

From: Comrade Alfred Wada <alfredwada_ecowas1@maktoob.com>
Date: Thursday, September 26, 2002, 22:08:35
Subject: urgent business cooperation

OVER INVOICED!

Honourable Director,

I am Comrade Alfred Wada, the Deputy Chairman of the Contract Awarding Committee of the Economic Community of West African States (ECOWAS) headquarters in Lome, Republic of Togo. I got your contact from the Togolaise Chamber of Commerce and Industries. In view of your profile I was mandated by my colleagues to contact you immediately for this mutual business relationship which involved a transfer of the sum of U.S.$18,300,000.00 (eighteen million three hundred thousand United States dollars only) into your personal or company's bank account for safe-keeping and subsequent disbursement among us.

This fund was a residue of the over invoiced contract bills awarded by us for the supply of military hard/softwares, medical items, light and heavy duty vehicles, apparels and other administrative logistics for the ECOMOG in Sierra Leone and Liberia during the peace keeping contingency.

As the deputy chairman of CAC, I have the cooperation and mandate of the financial director and the secretary of the organization to overinflate the values of the contracts awarded to different companies from different countries during the crisis. It was our consensus to seek the assistance of a willing foreigner to provide us with the facilities to transfer this money out of West Africa. This is born out of our belief in the non-stable and sporous political nature of this subregion.

The original contractors have been duly paid and this inflated value is awaiting claims by any foreign company of our choice. We intend to pay out this fund now as the organization is winding up its activities since the aim of returning peace to the countries and the coast has been achieved.

We need your assistance to provide an account for the transfer and your comprehensive advice, assistance and partnership for investment in your country. It is however agreed, as the account owner in this deal to allow you 30% of the entire sum as compensation, 65% will be held on trust for us while 5% will be used to defray any incidental expenses during the course of the transaction. Upon the receipt of acceptance, the text of the application of claim will be sent to you for transcription and forwarded to the organization for ratification and approvals for the immediate payment.

As with the case of all organized (sensitive) and conspired deals, we solicit your unreserved confidentiality and utmost secret in this business. We hope to retire peacefully and lead an honourable business life afterwards. There are no risks involved. I look forward to hear from you immediately.

Best regards,
Comrade Alfred Wada

Peace Keeping

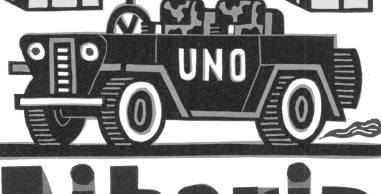

ECOMOG

UNO

Liberia

PROVIDE YOUR BANK ACCOUNT!

Dear Sir,

permit me to inform you of my desire of going into business relationship with you. I got your contact from the internet. I prayed over it and selected your name among other names. I am James Kone, the only son of late Mr. and Mrs. David Kone. My father was a very wealthy cocoa merchant in Abidjan, the economic capital of Ivory Coast before he was poisoned to death by his business associates on one of their outings to discuss on a business deal. When my mother died on the 21st October 1984, my father took me and my junior brother special because we were motherless.

Before the death of my father on 30th June 2000 in a private hospital here in Abidjan, he secretly called me on his bedside and told me that he has a sum of $12,500,000 (twelve million five hundred thousand dollars) left in a suspense account in a local bank here in Abidjan. He used my name as his first son for the next of kin in depositing of the fund. He also explained to me that it was because of this wealth and some huge amount of money, his business associates supposed to balance him from the deal they had and poisoned him. I should seek for a God fearing foreign partner in a country of my choice where I will transfer this money and use it for investment purpose, such as real estate management. Sir, we are honourably seeking your assistance in the following ways:

1) To provide a bank account where this money would be transferred to.
2) To serve as the guardian of this since I am a boy of 26 years.

Moreover Sir, we are willing to offer you 10% of the sum as compensation for effort input after the successful transfer of this fund to your designate account overseas.

Anticipating to hear from you soon.
Thanks and God bless.
Best regards,
James Kone

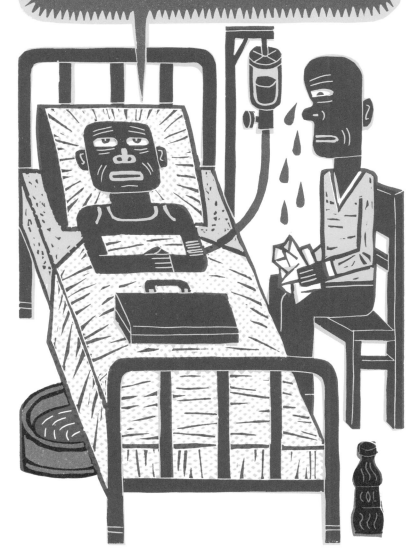

CONFIDENTIAL PROPOSAL

I am writing to solicit your assistance in executing a very profitable transaction. I got your contact from my boss' file. I work with an Ivorian based investment firm »a Mic« as the corporate affairs manager. In March 2001 I attended a business seminar in Bouaké, Côte d'Ivoire, where I was lucky to meet Alhaji Dangote, the president of Dangote Farm ets. Alhaji Dangote is an accomplished agriculturist who specialized in cattle farms. He has farms in different countries of West Africa. He is one of the greatest supplier of cattle, beef and other dairy products in this part of the world. Alhaji Dangote took me into confidence by informing me about the huge amount of money he spends on a particular medicine for his cattle. He buys this product at the rate of U.S.$5,000 per carton, to the excess of 300 cartons. He asked me if I could source a cheaper supplier considering the recent falls in the price of beef in the world.

Back to my office, I discussed this business proposal with my boss and he decided to handle the supply by himself. We carried out a market research and discovered that we could purchase this cattle medicine somewhere cheaper in Holland for U.S.$2,000 per carton. We moved a proposal to Mac Dowels to make a supply to him at U.S.$4,800 per carton which he accepted. Owing to my role in the whole arrangement, I had an agreement with my boss to be receiving 15% of whatever gain is made on each supply. But when the first supply of 120 cartons were made, my boss decided to renegade on our agreement. When I protested, he threatened to dismiss me from office. I decided to overlook this betrayal but since then our relationship has ceased to be cordial. He never said anything to me again about Dangote Farms ets. as I assumed that the business relationship has stopped between them.

But recently, I intercepted some letters from Alhaji Dangote to my boss. I was shocked to know that he has made three more supplies to Dangote farms ets. Now, Alhaji is requesting for supplies of 250 cartons of these substance following a suspected outbreak of disease among his cattle in Mali. These letters have not reached my boss and never will. Instead I called Alhaji Dangote and convinced him that I can supply him at the price of U.S.$4,400 per carton. But that he, Alhaji Dangote or his representative, will have to go to Holland and inspect it before lifting the goods. At the moment Alhaji Dangote is waiting for me or my foreign contact as he has agreed to stop all further dealings with my boss. If you can handle this project, please contact me immediately for details. I am ready to give you Alhaji's contact for your direct conversation with him.

Note: Alhaji Dangote must not know our purchasing source in Holland. If, he will not be needing our services anymore.

Thank you and God bless you,
Samuel Opute

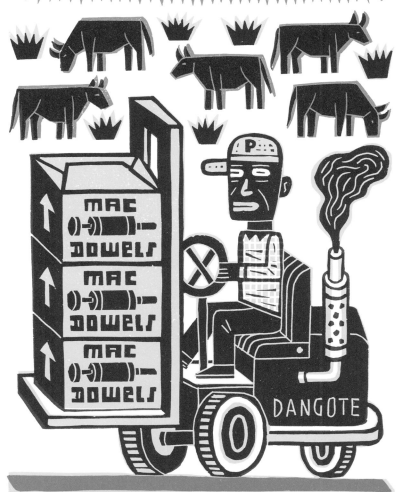

From: David Guei <daguei2611@netscape.net>
Date: Thursday, September 11, 2003, 12:40:57
Subject: thanks for your mail

URGENT AND CONFIDENTIAL ASSISTANCE

Dear Friend,

my name is David Guei, son of late General Robert Guei, the ex-military head of state of Ivory Coast, who was murdered along with the interior minister on the 19th of September 2002. You can visit http://news.bbc.co.uk/2/hi/africa/2269238. stm for complete report on this incident. I contacted you because of my need to deal with persons with whom my family and I have had no previous personal relationships.

Since the murder of my father, I have been subjected to all sorts of harassment and intimidation with lots of negative reports emanating from the government and the press about my family.

The present government has also ensured that our bank accounts are frozen and all assets seized. It is in view of this that I seek your assistance in the transfer of the sum of thirty million United States dollars (U.S.$30,000,000.00) being the very last of my family fund in my possession. After the murder of my father, the federal government seized all our properties and our accounts, both local and international were frozen.

My only hope now is the cash that my father carefully packaged and deposited as artifacts with a security company in Europe. The said sum can easily be withdrawn or paid to a recommended beneficiary. The security company based on my instructions will release the fund to you and you will be presented as my partner who will be fronting for me in areas of viable and profitable business.

To show my preparedness and appreciation to carry out this business with you, 25% of the total sum will be your share and 20% commission of the proceeds realized from the investment of this fund will also be yours, also 5% is to be set aside for any eventual cost that might arise as the transaction proceeds. I need your full cooperation for the success of this transaction.

I plead with you to treat this issue confidential and urgent because it is delicate and it demands a great degree of secrecy. I would want you to reach me through my e-mail address above if you are interested to assist me. I sincerely will appreciate your response. But right now, I am in South Africa as an asylum seeker.

I wait to hear from you.
Regards,
David Guei

MURDERED!
25% will be your share!

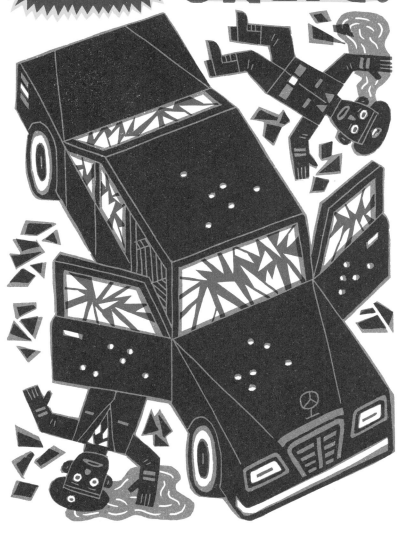

From: Stella M. Agyekum <stella_m_18@yahoo.com>
Date: Thuesday, September 23, 2003, 10:56:21
Subject: assistance

REVEAL THE TREASURE

Dear,

my name is Stella M. Agyekum. I am the only daughter of late Nana M. Agyekum, the traditional ruler of Bibiani before his death on 29th June 2003, after my mother's death on 21st October 1986.

It is my wish to inform you that presently I am in the Kwame Nkrumah University of Cape Coast Ghana the third year. Before the death of my father as a result of land dispute and also the death of my mother, my father has deposited 18 million United States dollars in a bank here in Accra, Ghana, in my name through a financial consultant. The firm has been taking care of me and recently a good lady friend of my late father who has also been helping me reveal to me about this treasure. With her I contacted the financial consultant firm and was taken to the bank to meet with the manager. The bank manager has cooperated with us and has paid off the financial firm as recorded in the agreement the firm entered with my father. Because of the land dispute that caused the death of my father I will not want to invest this money here in Ghana more over my age as a young girl.

This informed my soliciting for your assistance for the investment of this money. Any information you wish to know concerning this fund and myself will be given to you, including the bank to contact for the possible transfer of these funds to your chosen account.

Most importantly it is my wish to be adopted by you till I am matured. You will have 40% of the money.

God bless you while I wait for your urgent reply.
Stella M. Agyekum

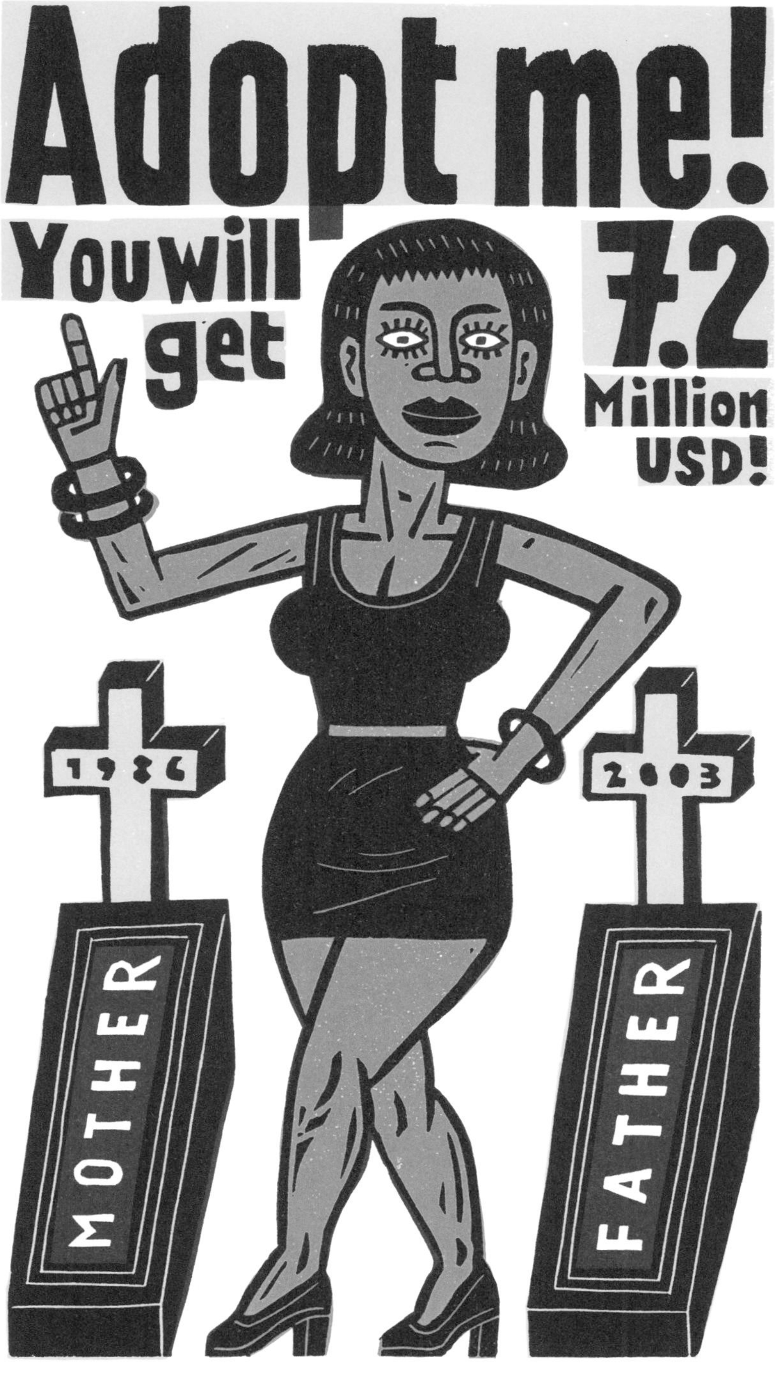

Adopt me!
You will get
7.2 Million USD!
1986
2003
MOTHER
FATHER

From: Kenneth Masuku <masukuproblem@netscape.net>
Date: Friday, April 23, 2004, 15:31:06
Subject: assist us

I NEED YOUR TRUSTWORTHINESS

Dear friend,

I wish to begin by way of introduction. I am Kenneth Masuku, the first and only surviving son of late Marc Masuku, one of the foremost and rich black farmers in Zimbabwe recently murdered in the land dispute in my country. Before the death of my father, he had given me the certificate of deposit of the sum of U.S.$30.5 million (thirty million five hundred United States dollars) in one of the private security companies in Europe, as family valuables, when he realized the looming dangers in Zimbabwe.

This amount was meant for the purchase of new machineries and chemicals for the farms and also for the establishment of new farms in Swaziland. The land dispute started when President Robert Mugabe introduced a new land reform, which was particularly targeted at the rich white farmers and a few black farmers (my father included).

This resulted in the gruesome killing of rich farmers (mainly whites) and the unlawful occupation of their properties by Mugabe's war veterans, under the disguise of fighting for the interest of the country. It is against this background that I fled the country with my family to the Netherlands where we are currently seeking asylum.

I have decided to seek foreign assistance, as the Netherlands law prohibits asylum seekers from operating bank accounts or involve in financial transaction of any kind, hence this letter to you. All I need is your trustworthiness to be able to entrust the above said amount and help me with investment opportunities. My family's survival depends on this money as we have virtually lost all our assets.

There are two options, firstly, you can choose to accept 15% of the total amount for your assistance or go into partnership for the proper investment of the money in your country.

We shall discuss in detail the modalities involved if you can reach me via this telephone number: 0031647988965 or via my confidential e-mail account. I await your reply through the above media, while I implore you to maintain the absolute secrecy required to ensure a safe and hitch free transaction. I shall furnish you with more details on request.

Yours truly,
Kenneth Masuku

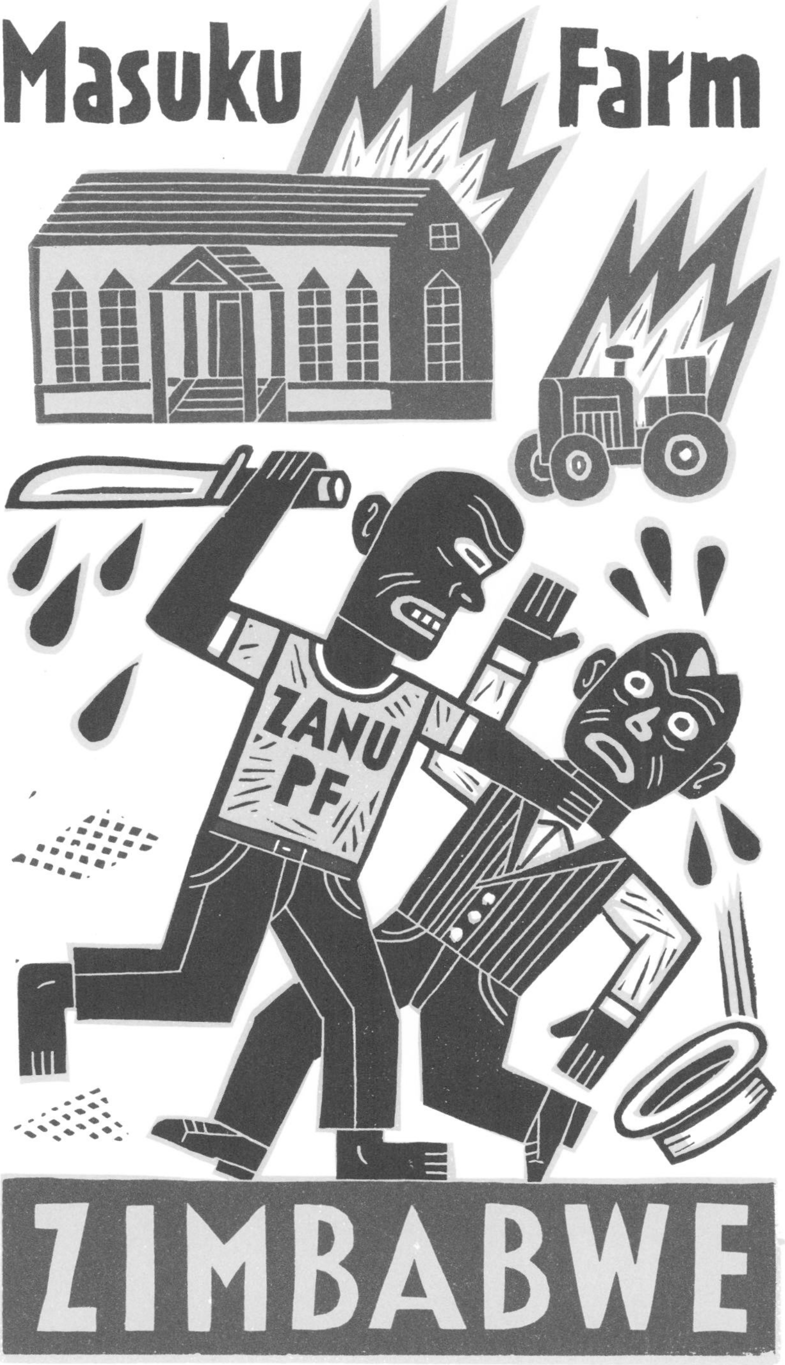
Masuku Farm
ZANU PF
ZIMBABWE

From: Frank Turner <frankturner41@hotmail.com>
Date: Friday, March 7, 2003, 21:26:14
Subject: I need your assistance.

ATTN. THE DIRECTOR/CEO

With due respect, trust and humility, I write this letter to seek your assistance though it is difficult since we have not had any correspondence before. I got your contact through the South African Information Exchange (S.A.I.E.) regarding your personal and business profile and I sincerely believe that you are capable to handle this urgent and international transaction.

I am Frank Turner, the son of Dr. Howard Turner, a Zimbabwean white farmer and businessman who was kidnapped early this year by dissident militants suspected to have the backing of the incumbent President Mugabe because of my father's outspokenness against his decision to seize white owned farms and give them to blacks without compensating the original white owners in order to secure votes in the past elections.

Four days after my father was kidnapped, he managed to sneak a written message to me and my brother, explaining his condition and one diplomatic box he deposited with the security company here in South Africa which contained the sum of U.S.$35.8 million (thirty five million eight hundred thousand United States dollars). But the content of the box was not disclosed to the security company due to security reasons. This money was contributed by his white colleagues of the Movement for Democratic Change of Zimbabwe (MDC) to battle president Mugabe should he try to manipulate the results in this past elections, since Zimbabweans are tired of his leadership. However, he was still able to manipulate the election and for this my family is not safe.

My father instructed us to move out of Zimbabwe for our safety, which we successfully did and now we are in South Africa. And because of the existing laws in South Africa, which bar asylum seekers/refugees like us to operate an account that exceeds U.S.$5,000.00 (five thousand United States dollars). This is where we seriously and urgently need your assistance for this money to be transferred into your account pending our arrival to your country. It is very important you understand that this transaction is 100% risk free, as no other source knows about this fund and our whereabouts.

As for your reward for your kind assistance, we have agreed to give you 18% of the total sum and 2% mapped out for any expenses we might incur during the course of the transfer and we intend to use 80% for investment in your country. Finally, I urge you to promise that you will not sit on this money when finally transferred into your account. Our lives depend on this fund as we do not know what future holds for us since our father and mother died a year ago. Please notify me on my above telephone or fax numbers if you intend helping us out.
I await your urgent reply.

Best regards,
Frank Turner

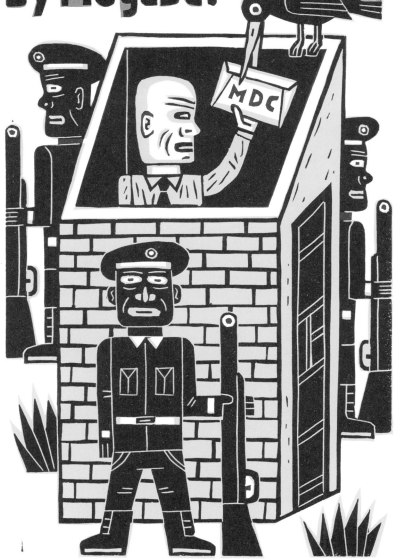

From: Taofeek Savimbi <taofeek1@voila.fr>
Date: Monday, March 10, 2003, 15:20:17
Subject: help my familiy!

HELP MY FAMILY

This letter may come to you as a surprise due to the fact that we have not met. The message could be strange but real, if you pay some attention to it. I could have notified you about it at least for the sake of your integrity. Please accept my sincere apologies. In bringing this message of goodwill to you, I have to say that I have no intention of causing you any pain.

I am Mr. Taofeek Savimbi, son of the late rebel leader Jonas Savimbi of Angola who was killed on the 22nd of February 2002. I managed to get your contact details through the internet myself. Time is of importance and I was desperately looking for a person to assist me in this confidential business.

My late father, Jonas Savimbi, was able to deposit a large sum of money in different security vaults in Europe. My father is dead and the movement of his family members (including me) is restricted. We are forbidden to travel out of our localities. Presently our movements are monitored. Right now there is a rush for my father's wealth by the government who are claiming that most of the wealth was got by arms smuggling and therefore illegal. You can know more about my father by checking his profile at www.kwacha.com/edoc2.htm

His wealth has been estimated to be approximately U.S.$100 million and being close to my father I happen to be in possession of documents and information of some of the wealth. Only my trusted mother knows that I have this information. Presently, there are U.S.$50,000,000.00 (fifty million dollars) cash and precious materials my father moved to Europe before his death, deposited in a security vault. Before you can get access to it I have to give you the necessary documents, the password to the vault and power of attorney to allow you to the vault.

I am therefore soliciting your help to travel to Amsterdam in Europe to receive this money and transfer in bits into your account before my government gets wind of the funds. You know my father was a rebel leader in Angola before his death. My reason for doing this is because it will be difficult for the Angolan government to trace my father's money to an individual's account that has no relationship with the Savimbi family. I am currently and temporarily living in South Africa as a refugee. I intend to communicate with you in regards of this transaction via the internet and telephone but my access to communication facilities at this point is restricted.

When you are ready I will give you the information needed before you can get access to the 2kg of AU gold, 85g of pure diamond and raw cash of U.S.$50 million American dollars. You will then proceed to Holland for the collection. Please your confidentiality in this transaction is highly required. I await your response.

Yours sincerely
Taofeek Savimbi

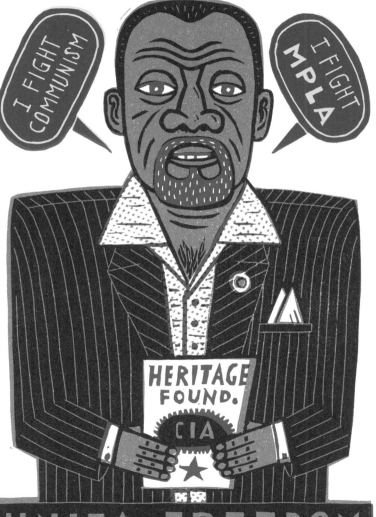

From: Eduado de Mello <jsed@hkem.com>
Date: Thursday, May 23, 2002, 10:04:43
Subject: cooperation

MY INHERITANCE

Dear Sir,

I am Mr. Eduado de Mello, one of the principal commanders of the Union for the Total Independence of Angola, UNITA. Well, needless telling a very long story here. Our story is indeed interwoven with the history of the world and the liberation struggle in the southern region of the African continent. The bubble burst just some weeks ago when my supreme commander, the late Dr. Jonas Savimbi was killed in an encounter with the forces of the MPLA government. The rest is now history but suffice it to say that I am tired of the unfortunate role of waging a war against my fatherland. I have therefore decided to pull out my troupes from the bush even if the other field commanders decide otherwise.

I am poised to effect a new beginning in my life and I have decided to make South Africa my new home at least for the interim period until I am sufficiently sure that I would be welcome home whole-heartedly by the MPLA government in Luanda.

Needles to say I was the single most important commander to the late supreme commander Dr. Jonas Savimbi. Indeed because I am a brother to one of his wives, he confided in me a great deal. He sent me to deposit the sum of thirty two million dollars (U.S.$32 million) with a security company in South Africa. This was immediately after the events of September 11, 2001 in the United States of America. Indeed it has become increasingly difficult to move large volumes of money around the world particularly for a liberation movement like UNITA, hence the recourse to keeping the money with the security company in South Africa. I have decided to inherit this money which was deposited as cash in hundred dollar denominations. The money is kept in my signature and would have been used in the purchase of arms and ammunition for the purposes of continuing the civil war in Angola. As already stated I have decided to quit the whole thing.

I want to cooperate with you in my decision to inherit the $32 million. I am still in the bush here but I have been able to establish contact with the security company in South Africa. Note also that I deposited the money as a foreign national who is the head of a mining company in Angola (never as a commander of UNITA).

If you are able to cooperate with me over this I am willing to give you 20% of the $32 million. The security company is standing by to receive my instructions on this and I will link you up with them as soon as you are ready to take possession of the $32 million. Finally you are to note that in your reply, you are to state your residential or company address and if possible send a copy of your international passport so as to assure me that my money is safe in your hands.

Yours truly,
Eduado de Mello

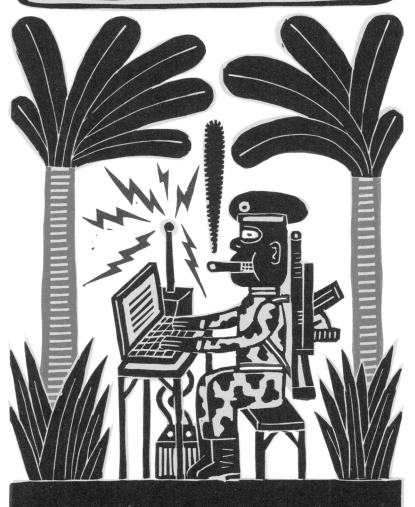

I NEED YOUR ASSISTANCE

Dear friend,
it is a pleasure to contact you at this important time for a possible business transaction. However, I got your contact through a search on the internet web site and your profile got me convinced of your wide experience in business.

I am Ms. Agnes Kobe Savimbi, the daughter of the late General Jonas Savimbi, leader of the Angolan UNITA rebels who was shot dead on Tuesday 26th February 2002 by the opposing forces of the Angolan army. For the past years now our country has been in political crisis and conflicts between the UNITA rebels and government allied forces.

I am writing you based on the following reason: before the death of General Jonas Savimbi, I was given U.S.$10.8 million dollars, 45,550 carat diamond and 5400 ounce gold for the purchasing of fire arms and ammunition from Russia and a mini frigate from Ukraine. I considered it a great opportunity as he is now late, confiscated the package and diverted it to Abidjan, Côte d'Ivoire, West Africa, where it has been deposited in a security company on a special arrangement as family treasures.

Therefore, my aim of contacting you is for you to assist me with your personality and influence to move and secure the said amount and treasure over to your country, for safe keeping prior to when I will arrive in your country. I have the ambition of investing this money and as well keeping a long lasting fruitful relationship with you.

Presently, I am in Abidjan, capital city of Côte d'Ivoire, West Africa, where I have been in hideout for the past three weeks since I was sent on this assignment before his death. I would like to appeal to you that time is not my friend as I am anxiously looking forward for a responsible, reliable and honest person to act as my client or beneficiary so that I will transfer this treasure out of Africa, because I am not safe here.

Dear friend, if you can sincerely assist me concerning this transaction with all your trust, we shall discuss about your percentage share first as soon as I receive your urgent and positive reply. Please, kindly handle this proposal with your utmost secrecy and confidential as all the necessary documents and proves as regards to this treasure will be forwarded to you on your request. Hoping that our transaction will be considered with utmost confidentiality, I will be expecting to receive your response as soon as you finish reading this mail.

Yours sincerely,
Ms. Agnes Kobe Savimbi

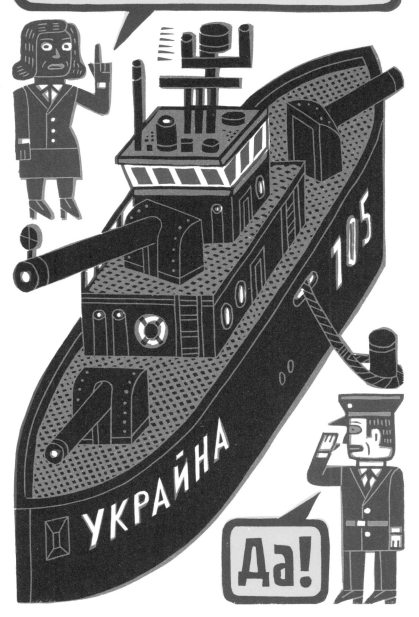

From: Alahaji Cyril <glareal g_global2002@yahoo.com>
Date: Monday, June 10, 2002, 08:29:37
Subject: message

URGENT PROPOSAL

Attention Director,
Dear Sir,
I am proposing this great business opportunity on behalf of Cyril Consulting Firm
Our organization is presently in charge with the responsibility of exporting and
selling of diamonds by our neighboring country head of state under a special and
secret arrangement.

Be informed that His Excellence decided to apply this strategy in order to avoid
attacking United Nations sanction against illegal supply of arms and ammunition
to rebels in exchange of diamonds. Note: the reason for withdrawal of names
and other relevant informations is due to security reasons. Of course you will be
duly informed as soon as you confirm you're genuinely interested and maybe also
provide you the privilege of meeting His Excellence in person if needed.

In a nutshell, we will be delighted to supply to your organization as much
quantity of diamonds at a reasonable price, in addition, we also have immunity to
supply these diamonds to you in a natural ground like Europe.

Please, if you are interested in our proposal/offer, kindly send us a reply or call
at tel. 225076833628.

Yours sincerely
Alahaji Cyril

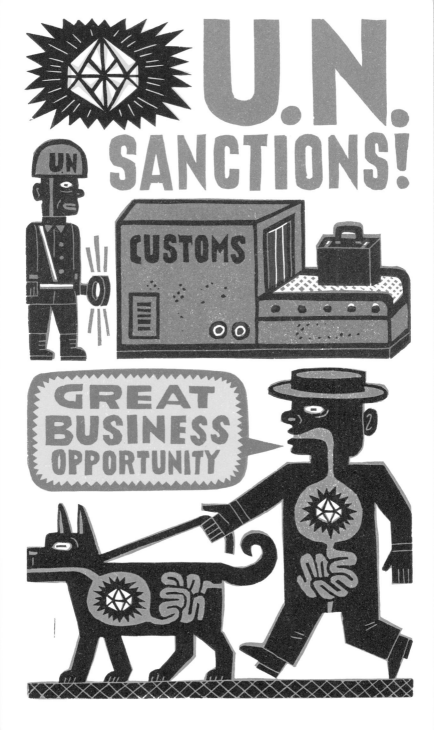

From: Ugo Olems <ugo2b@37.com>
Date: Tuesday, July 02, 2002, 02:08:37
Subject: urgent bussiness transaction

URGENT BUSINESS TRANSACTION

Dear Sir,

my name is Dr. Ugo Olems, Ghanaian national, married with a wife and four children. I work as an administrative secretary to Standard Security & Services Ltd. in Nigeria. I got your contact from the Ghanaian Chamber of Commerce and after due consultation with my spiritual adviser, I believe that by the grace of God you will accept to be my partner in this mutual business.

I have been working with this company for eleven good years. Within this period, I have watched with meticulous precision how African heads of state have been using Standard Security to move huge sums of U.S. dollars, pounds sterling, french francs to their foreign partners oversea. They bring in these consignments of money cash and secretly declare the contents as jewelry, gold, diamonds, precious stones, family treasures, documents etc. Gen. Sani Abacha of Nigeria (dead), Mobutu Sese Seko of Zaire (dead), Foday Sankoy of Siera Leone, Rtd. Gen. Ibrahim Babangida of Nigeria, Felix Houphet Buigny of Ivory Coast (dead), Kanan Bedie of Ivory Coast etc. have tens of consignments deposited with us. Their foreign partners claim most of the consignments. But a lot of them are laying here unclaimed for as much as two years now. Nobody may ever come for them because the documents of deposit are never available to anybody except the depositors.

In Standard Security the procedure of claims is as soon as you are able to produce the secret information of a consignment, it will be released to you upon demand. From my record, more than four consignments belonging to Mobutu Sese Seko have been claimed in the past six months. This is why I am soliciting for your cooperation. Late Gen. Sani Abacha has five consignments deposited with several codes. One has been claimed in the past two years. Since he died, the family members are under restricted arrest without communication, some ran into exile. I have finished every arrangement for you to claim consignment No. 002101 containing U.S.$45,000,000.00. My duty is to supply you with all the information needed to claim the consignment. The procedure is very simple and easy:

Apply officially to the Director of Operations of Standard Security for the release of consignment No. 002101. The management will demand for documents and secret codes of the consignment. I will supply you with every detailed information needed. As soon as they confirm it to be correct they will invite you for the collection. Please, nobody should ever know I am involved in the deal except the lawyer who will write an agreement bond for us.

I will suggest upon conclusion, we share 70% for me, 20% for you and 10% for any expenses incurred during the course of the transfer. I assure you that this deal has been carefully hatched for months. I bet my life that we cannot fail.

Dr. Ugo Olems.

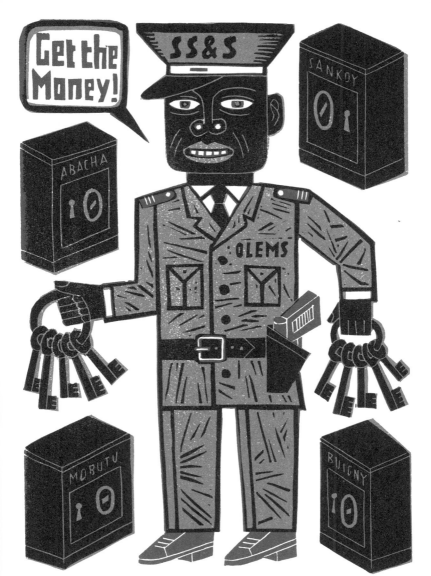

From: Patrick King Elsworth <pk_elsworth@yahoo.com>
Date: Monday, June 17, 2002, 03:09:03
Subject: urgent assistance required...not a scam

NOT A SCAM

This letter is not intended to cause you any embarrassment. Following knowledge of your high repute and trustworthiness, it is borne out of this difficult situation that our family has been engulfed out since my father and bread winner of the family was forced to relinquish from his position.

However, I know that your immediate apprehensions may be as a result of the popular scam reports. I must reiterate that you must not swallow hook, line and sinker of all that you have been told. We are aware of these reports about scam. Most African countries have been famed for such activities.

My dear, the truth is that many people remain poor in life because of their ignorance of certain privilege information. A lot of people have unwittingly blown several privilege opportunities because they choose to leave the veil over their face and swallow the hook, line and sinker, the sponsored media sold to them, which is exactly what they aim to achieve. It's really very pathetic that your problem after gone through this mail will be fear, an almost all-consuming fear of the unknown. You are afraid that something might go wrong.

In life, dreams and fears go hand in hand. Even the most courageous men on earth have their own fears, but courage means being able to perform in the midst of fear. It is said that an individual cannot discover new oceans until he has the courage to lose sight of the shores. Do not fear or despair, as this transaction has no bearing or any relation with scam, we presently have found ourselves (men of great hope and aspiration) in the most trying times where because of insufficient resources, little minds tend to spite us, but there is a dawn of hope, we have toiled all night, we can not give in to human dissuasions, history has a place for minds of steel. When they first manufactured golf balls, they made the cover smooth. Then it was discovered that after a ball had been roughened up one could get more distance out of it. So it is with life, it takes some rough spots in your life to make you go your farthest.

My name is Mr. Patrick King Elsworth, the son of Mr. Henry Elsworth of Zimbabwe. During the current war crisis against the farmers in Zimbabwe President Robert Mugabe ordered to invade my father's farm and burn everything as much as killing my beloved father. Before his death, my father deposited the sum of U.S.$15.5 million for 285 acres of new farm land in Shiselweni Village near Umbuluzi river in Swaziland, negotiated to buy with the help of the monarch King Suboza Mswati III. as well as buying tractors from New London Tractor & Equipment, Route 460 West of Lynchburg, London.

The U.N.H.C.R. advised me to contact you to move this money out of here for investment in your country. Would you be kind enough to assist me? I do not have any knowledge of international business. Thanks and best regards,

Patrick King Elsworth

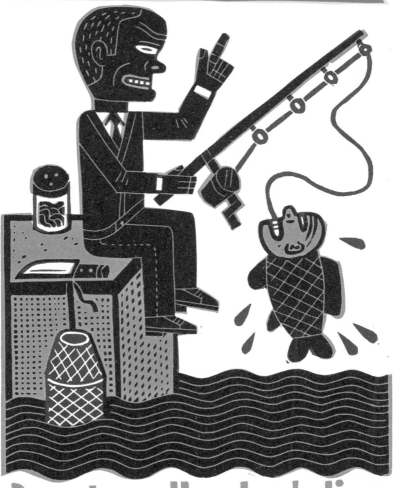

Thanks to Jonathan Lutes for the translation of the foreword
and Sophie Zeitz for editing the emails.
First Published in the United States of America, 2006
First Edition

Gingko Press, Inc.
5768 Paradise Drive, Suite J
Corte Madera, CA 94925, USA
Phone (415) 924 9615 / Fax (415) 924 9608

email: books@gingkopress.com
www.gingkopress.com

ISBN: 1-58423-245-5
ISBN 13: 978-1-58423-245-2

Typeset in: Akzidenz Grotesk Bold and Bold Condensed
Printed in Hong Kong